The Maya Civilization

An Enthralling Overview of Maya History, Starting from the Olmecs' Domination of Ancient Mexico to the Arrival of Hernan Cortes and the Spanish Conquest

© Copyright 2021

The content contained within this book may not be reproduced, duplicated, or transmitted without direct written permission from the author or the publisher.

Under no circumstances will any blame or legal responsibility be held against the publisher, or author, for any damages, reparation, or monetary loss due to the information contained within this book, either directly or indirectly.

Legal Notice:

This book is copyright protected. It is only for personal use. You cannot amend, distribute, sell, use, quote, or paraphrase any part, or the content within this book, without the consent of the author or publisher.

Disclaimer Notice:

Please note the information contained within this document is for educational and entertainment purposes only. All effort has been executed to present accurate, up-to-date, reliable, complete information. No warranties of any kind are declared or implied. Readers acknowledge that the author is not engaging in the rendering of legal, financial, medical, or professional advice. The content within this book has been derived from various sources. Please consult a licensed professional before attempting any techniques outlined in this book.

By reading this document, the reader agrees that under no circumstances is the author responsible for any losses, direct or indirect, that are incurred due to the use of the information contained within this document, including, but not limited to, errors, omissions, or inaccuracies.

Free limited time bonus

Stop for a moment. We have a free bonus set up for you. The problem is this: we forget 90% of everything that we read after 7 days. Crazy fact, right? Here's the solution: we've created a printable, 1-page pdf summary for this book that you're reading now. All you have to do to get your free pdf summary is to go to the following website: **https://livetolearn.lpages.co/enthrallinghistory/**

Once you do, it will be intuitive. Enjoy, and thank you!

Contents

INTRODUCTION 1
PART ONE: THE OLMECS AND PRECLASSIC MAYA
(1400BC-250 AD) 4
    CHAPTER 1: SAN LORENZO TENOCHTITLAN: THE CITY OF
    THE OLMECS 5
    CHAPTER 2: LA VENTA: THE OLMEC ISLAND CITY 16
    CHAPTER 3: OLMEC DECLINE AND THE EPI-OLMECS 29
    CHAPTER 4: THE PRECLASSIC MAYA ERA 36
PART TWO: THE CLASSIC MAYA ERA (250-900 AD) 49
    CHAPTER 5: CLASSIC MAYA SOCIETY 50
    CHAPTER 6: TIKAL: THE MAYA JAGUAR GOD CITY 69
    CHAPTER 7: CALAKMUL: THE LOST MAYA EMPIRE 81
    CHAPTER 8: THE COLLAPSE OF THE CLASSIC ERA 91
    CHAPTER 9: CHICHEN ITZA: THE WONDER CITY 96
PART THREE: THE POSTCLASSIC MAYA ERA (900-1511 AD) ... 106
    CHAPTER 10: THE K'ICHE' KINGDOM OF Q'UMARKAJ 107
    CHAPTER 11: THE LEAGUE OF MAYAPAN 112
    CHAPTER 12: PETEN ITZA: THE LAST MAYA KINGDOM 116
PART FOUR: SPANISH CONTACT AND CONQUEST
(1511-1697 AD) 122
    CHAPTER 13: FIRST ENCOUNTERS AND YUCATAN
    EXPLORATION 123

CHAPTER 14: HERNAN CORTES AND PEDRO DE
ALVARADO 131
CHAPTER 15: CONQUEST OF THE CHIAPAS 141
CHAPTER 16: CONQUEST OF THE YUCATAN PENINSULA........ 149
CHAPTER 17: THE FINAL CONQUESTS 155
CONCLUSION... 157
HERE'S ANOTHER BOOK BY ENTHRALLING HISTORY
THAT YOU MIGHT BE INTERESTED IN 160
FREE LIMITED TIME BONUS 161
BIBLIOGRAPHY:.. 162

Introduction

The Maya are one of the most captivating civilizations of Mesoamerican history, with monumental architecture and distinctive artwork is still marveled at today. While popular media has often portrayed the Maya as primitive peoples that revolved around gruesome human sacrifice, they were one of the world's most advanced civilizations during their height of power.

This book aims to inform the reader on the realities of the Maya civilization, from its beginnings on the Gulf Coast to the arrival of the Spanish conquistadors on the Yucatan Peninsula. While no one will ever truly understand the extent of Maya history and culture, this book will use a variety of resources to give a general overview of the timeline of the civilization.

Part one will explore the Olmec, often called the "mother civilization" of the advanced Mesoamerican civilizations that came after it. The breathtaking architectural and artistic achievements, as well as their political and scientific advancements, will be covered. These chapters will largely focus on the Olmec cities of San Lorenzo and La Venta, as well as the Epi-Olmec city of Tres Zapotes. In the concluding chapter of part one, the Preclassic Maya period will be explored: a time period of enormous transformation and growth in the Maya heartland as Olmec society was declining.

Part two will cover the Classic Maya period when the Maya civilization was the dominating force of Central America. First, the Classic urban Maya society will be explored. This will cover their fascinating religious beliefs, their concept of time, and much, much more. These chapters will largely focus on the two largest cities of the Maya lowlands during the classic period, Tikal and Calakmul. The collapse of the Classic Maya city-states and the many theories of why the collapse occurred will then be covered, as well as the rise of cities in the northern Yucatan, namely Chichen Itza.

Part three will revolve around the Postclassic period, as the populations and political and domination of the lowland urban centers dispersed throughout the Yucatan region. The K'iche' Maya of the highlands, the Mayapan league of the northern Yucatan, and the kingdom of Peten Itza of the lowlands will be covered. This will give the reader a great foundation for what Maya society looked like upon the arrival of the Spanish conquistadors.

Part four will explore the decades of Spanish conquest that enveloped the Yucatan region. The numerous conquistadors, their expeditions, and how they affected local Maya populations will be covered.

While this book aims to be comprehensive, many great cities and components of Maya life will surely be left out. However, its text serves as a great starting point for readers that are interested in further learning about one of the world's greatest civilizations.

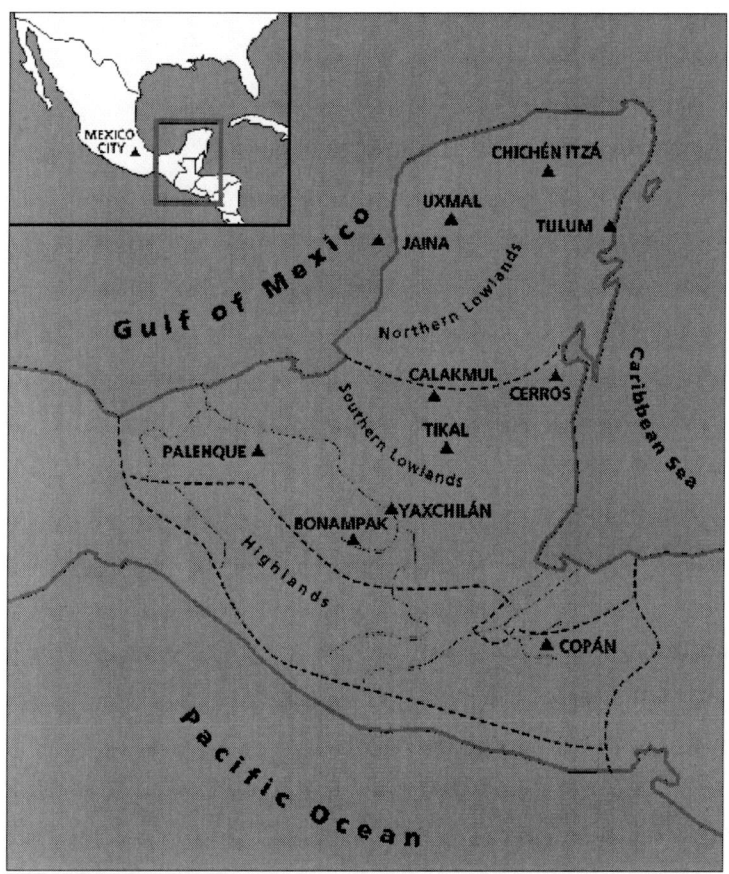

https://www.historymuseum.ca/cmc/exhibitions/civil/maya/mmc11eng.html

PART ONE: THE OLMECS AND PRECLASSIC MAYA (1400BC-250 AD)

Chapter 1: San Lorenzo Tenochtitlan: The City of the Olmecs

The Olmecs are widely considered the first civilization of Mesoamerica and one of the most prominent "mother cultures" that would eventually become the great Mayan and Aztec civilizations. Up until the 13th century BC, ancient Mesoamerica was largely comprised of small primitive villages scattered throughout Central America. The Olmecs advanced far past the confines of a primitive stone-age civilization and eventually became the dominating people of the Gulf Coast region of southern Mexico.

The Olmecs were exceptional sculptors, and their art would prove highly influential to the Mesoamerican civilizations that emerged in Central America after them. The sculptures and architecture of the Olmecs have proved to be indispensable to understanding their ancient culture, as these stone artifacts have been some of the only traces of the Olmecs that have survived. Not only were they talented sculptors and artisans, but they proved to be excellent administrators, agriculturalists, and diplomats.

The Olmecs expanded on primitive farming villages and created great agricultural city centers, where advanced irrigation and farming methods were used. The first of these city centers was San Lorenzo Tenochtitlan, located around 38 miles away from the Gulf of Mexico in the modern-day state of Veracruz. (This city is not to be confused with the Aztec capital of Tenochtitlan that would emerge many centuries later.)

The yellow dots show known Olmec villages and towns. The red dots mark locations where artifacts or art have been found that are unassociated with habitation. (Credit: Wikimedia Commons)

San Lorenzo is considered the first advanced Olmec city and was by far the most prosperous city of the region during Mesoamerican history's Early Formative period (1800-900 BC). The city became the dominating power of the Gulf Coastal Plain, which helped Olmec culture spread widely into other Mesoamerican societies.

Olmec society was thriving in the region for hundreds of years before the creation of San Lorenzo. The nearby El Manatí site had been in use since 1600 BC and prospered as a small coastal town. The archaeology of the site shows that Olmec settlers began arriving in the area of San Lorenzo around 1450 BC, and it increasingly grew into a large village.

However, it was not until the ascension of San Lorenzo as the dominating power of the region in the 12th century BC that the use of hunting and gathering practices, agriculture, distinctive Olmec culture, and administrative skill all came together to form an advanced Mesoamerican city center.

The city had a socioeconomic political structure that greatly resembled ancient city-states in Europe and Asia, consisting of elite landowners and a peasant working class. The extensive trade networks that connected the city's economy to other Mesoamerican communities throughout the region greatly aided the diffusion of different cultures throughout Central America.

Between 1150 and 900 BC, San Lorenzo enjoyed its peak of dominance in the region until it was eventually replaced as the regional power by the nearby Olmec city of La Venta. By the beginning of the 9th century BC, much of San Lorenzo's population had moved elsewhere. Though there would be later settlements in the city, it would never come close to the prosperity it once possessed. Many scholars speculate that this mass dispersal and exodus of San Lorenzo's population laid the groundwork for the Maya Civilization that would dominate the region years later.

The first excavations of the San Lorenzo site began in 1945 by Mathew Stirling and Philip Drucker, sponsored by the Smithsonian Institute and National Geographic Society. Stirling uncovered many of the first remnants of the Olmec city and greatly surprised the archaeological community by declaring that the city belonged to an ancient civilization that predated the Maya.

However, most of his findings were from 600 to 400 BC, long past the city's golden age. In 1966, Michael Coe led the Yale University Project into the city's ruins, and massive excavation mapping projects were conducted, showing the true timeline of the Olmec city. The San Lorenzo Tenochtitlan Archaeological Project has directed the city's excavation since 1990, and its work has led to the discovery of thousands of artifacts, monuments, and settlement patterns.

City Landscape

The city was located in one of Mesoamerica's largest coastal regions. It was built on elevated ground (160 feet high) surrounded by a plain – including numerous tributaries and water sources. The city's location on elevated ground greatly increased its population density, as people located throughout the wetlands moved to the city to escape flooding. The city's central area covered around 140 acres, and it is estimated that the Olmecs moved between 50,000 and 2,000,000 cubic meters of dirt by basket to build the city.

An estimated 5,500 people could have lived in the immediate city, while 13,000 people could have populated the entire surrounding region. During the city's height, it controlled much of the Coatzacoalcos River basin. However, many areas to the north and east of the city enjoyed considerable autonomy from San Lorenzo's influence, including the city of La Venta.

Fishing, hunting, and gathering throughout the coastal floodplain of the city was the main form of sustenance for the city's population during its initial rise to power. Snook was the primary fish caught by San Lorenzo's fishermen, and aquatic animals made up around 60% of the city's meat consumption. The city also relied on many non-aquatic species for food, such as deer, birds, dogs, and rabbits.

While the city's population initially obtained most of its food from floodplain resources, it increasingly began to rely on agriculture throughout the Early Formative period. An estimated 30 square miles of the region were set aside to cultivate the primary crop of the Olmecs: maize. The city's inhabitants could produce 500 metric tons of maize every year, feeding around 5,500 people. While much of its agricultural sector was devoted to maize production, beans and manioc – a woody shrub also known as yuca – were widely harvested throughout the region.

The city's agricultural land was prosperous because of the region's heavy rainfall and the rich soil nurtured by the Gulf Coast and its numerous water sources. Competition for these fertile soils created competition amongst the city's population, which laid the foundations for San Lorenzo's socioeconomic composition. An elite landowning class was created in the city due to this competition, and the economic system of San Lorenzo increasingly mirrored the systems of many European and Asian kingdoms.

While the ruling elite resided on the elevated plateau of the city, most of the population lived on the plateau's slope. The ruling class lived in large houses built on platforms made of clay, with many of the city's distinctive statues surrounding their houses.

The "Red Palace," which was reserved for the city's most elite, was made of dirt floors and walls that were plastered with sand and stained by hematite. The palace was a complex that included five different structures and a large workshop dedicated to basalt sculptures. Other elite houses were made with basalt, clay, limestone, or mud.

Outside of San Lorenzo, many other nearby settlements and villages were under the direct influence of the city. The nearby settlements of Tenochtitlan and Potrero Nuevo were populated by peasants and farmers that were a central part of the city's agricultural production. These small villages were most likely ruled by elite members of the city's population. These smaller communities were not only used for agricultural production to feed the city's population but also to act as military garrisons for the city's defense.

This shows that San Lorenzo was much more than an agrarian Olmec city. During its peak of power, San Lorenzo became a regional empire that used its surrounding area to further strengthen itself.

The city's engineers also created a sophisticated drainage system. A horseshoe-shaped drainage system comprised of pipes that were made from stone brought water in and out. Some evidence points to water having a ceremonial and religious value in Olmec culture, as many of these water systems were decorated with spiritual inscriptions and objects. The city also built dikes to control flooding around the rivers at Potrero Nuevo and El Azuzul.

Sculptures

The city is famous in the field of archaeology due to the many stone statues and sculptures that have been found throughout the ruins there. The most famous style of these sculptures has been named the "colossal heads."

San Lorenzo Colossal Head 3. This particular head weighs around 9 tons and measures 5.8 feet high and 5.3 feet wide. (Credit: Maribel Ponce Iba; frida27ponce)

The largest of these statues was nine feet tall, with some weighing as much as 28 tons. The heads were usually depicted with headgear that resembles the helmets of early 20th-century American football.

These statues are believed to represent supernatural beings of the Olmec religion, leaders of the city, or revered ancestors of the city's families. Archaeologists have discovered many of these sculptures throughout the San Lorenzo site, and it is believed that there are many more scattered throughout the region. Archaeology has shown that the city was the location for many ceremonies and rituals, and these sculptures were a prominent part of many of the ceremonies.

Even more impressive than the heads themselves is the method in which they were built. Like many other Olmec artifacts, they were built with basaltic rocks. Builders of the statues would travel to the Tuxtla Mountains 40 miles away to retrieve basalt from the Cerro Cinotepeque volcano. It is thought that the stones were dragged to the Coatzacoalcos River, where they were transported by raft to the city. This shows the great sophistication of the Olmecs, as this would not have been an easy feat.

The sculptors of the city created not only giant head sculptures but also smaller depictions of regional animals. During the early stages of the city's ascension to regional power, animals were frequently used in Olmec artwork, which may indicate that the animal world played an important role in their spirituality. The Olmec sculptors created a distinct style of figurines that depicted a jaguar-human hybrid. Clay ceramic pottery was produced and used throughout San Lorenzo households, and archaeological evidence suggests that ceramics were widely exported out of the city.

An adolescent presenting a were-jaguar baby. It is 22 inches tall and is the largest known greenstone sculpture. (Credit: Mag2017)

Sculptor and ceramic workshops were run by the elite, and the artwork was largely used to legitimize and maintain the authority of San Lorenzo's highest-class citizens. The sculptures were strategically placed throughout the city at entrances, large plazas, and outside the homes of the elite.

The inhabitants of San Lorenzo were avid traders, frequently trading with neighboring cities and settlements. Obsidian, which was largely used to build weapons and farming equipment, was bought from nine different Mesoamerican sources throughout the highlands of southern Mexico and Guatemala.

Olmec pottery that was created in the city has been found at archaeological sites throughout Central America, especially in the Chiapas state on the modern-day Mexico-Guatemalan border. In fact, more Olmec objects were found at the Canton Corralito site in Chiapas than in the city of San Lorenzo itself. The city mainly exported these objects, as there has been no evidence found at the San Lorenzo site of the city importing pottery or other ceramic objects from outside cultures.

Most of the sculptures were destroyed or damaged around 900 BC, the time period when the city began its steep decline. While experts have not reached a consensus on the exact reason for its decline, the destruction of the sculptures may point to either the conquering of the city by an invading force or a population abandoning it – symbolically destroying all that it stood for.

A ceramic bird-shaped vessel; note the red ochre (a clay pigment). This piece has been dated between the 13th century and the 9th century BC. It can be seen in the Metropolitan Museum of Art, New York, USA. (Credit: Wikimedia Commons)

Decline

From 1400 to 900 BC, San Lorenzo enjoyed its peak of power in the region, but from 900 BC to 400 BC, the population began to decline as the population increasingly moved out of the city. From 300 to 50 BC, the population declined even further until it was nearly deserted. The city was eventually repopulated sparsely from 800 to 1000 AD, but it never again reached anywhere close to what it once was.

Experts widely agree that the city declined and was replaced by La Venta as the regional power in the 10th century BC, but the cause of this rapid decline is unknown. The archaeological evidence shows that beginning around 900 BC, no more stone monuments or other large projects were constructed in the city. During this period, the population of the central plateau of the city declined by a staggering 57%.

Some have speculated that it was invaded by a rival city or deteriorated due to environmental changes. The shifting of the nearby ancient rivers away from the city may have severely disrupted the city's vital trade networks, and a drought that occurred during the time of the decline may have led to a decrease in crop yields.

Recent scholarship has shown evidence that throughout the Early Formative period, the city relied mostly on its coastal location for sustenance. Hunting and gathering throughout the floodplain brought many outsiders into the city, contributed to population growth, and created a political system that the elite used to maintain stability in the region. However, as the population increasingly began to rely on agriculture, this system may have begun to unravel.

The decline of San Lorenzo was most likely not caused by a single cataclysmic event but rather changing circumstances that caused its population to move elsewhere. The elite of the city surely relied on its populations' dependency on sustenance from the floodplain to maintain their control over the population, and this system of dependency may have been dismantled by an increased reliance on agriculture as the population increasingly moved into isolated farming villages in the uplands.

Some scholars believe this may indicate that the population of the city may have grown increasingly disillusioned by their government and were more than willing to move out of San Lorenzo when the opportunity presented itself. Others have surmised that the city's population simply saw more opportunity in living in isolated rural farming areas or in other surrounding settlements like La Venta that were increasingly growing more prosperous than San Lorenzo.

While San Lorenzo never again rose as a dominating city in the region after 900 BC, it laid the groundwork for the many Mesoamerican cities that would come after it. The success of the city as a regional power during the Early Formative period showed that the ever-growing developments of Mesoamerican technology, culture, and administration could no longer be confined to primitive Stone Age village society. The death of San Lorenzo as a regional power of the Gulf Coast marked the beginning of advanced Mesoamerican civilization in ancient Central America.

Chapter 2: La Venta: The Olmec Island City

The decline of San Lorenzo around 900 BC marked the neighboring city of La Venta's rise to power in the region. La Venta would enjoy half a millennium of regional dominance during the Middle Formative period (900-400 BC) of Mesoamerican history before it too was deserted by much of its population.

Throughout the Middle Formative period, influences from the city of San Lorenzo spread throughout Central America, as larger settlements and urban centers began to emerge throughout Mesoamerican society. The increased reliance on agriculture meant that Mesoamerican sustenance no longer relied on hunting and gathering, and the ownership of fertile land began to transform the power structures of the region.

As these towns grew, socioeconomic class structures were created, and elite members of cities increasingly demanded luxury items, including everything from stone figurines to blocks of serpentine. This created an explosion of Olmec crafts and artisanship, with many of the cities' elite actively creating workshops to produce these objects in mass. Trade networks throughout the region became used more frequently, as the demand for these items led to cities specializing in some production and importing others.

Not only did settlements grow by increased population density, but distinctive Olmec cultural practices also became more engrained in the region, as these city centers became hotbeds for a variety of Mesoamerican cultural influences. No other city better displayed this explosion of Olmec culture during the Middle Formative period than the city of La Venta.

Many archaeologists believe that La Venta was the largest Olmec city of ancient Mesoamerica, both in population and influence. Compared to the San Lorenzo site, excavations at La Venta indicate that the city ingrained religious ceremony much deeper in its population. City priests had enormous power in La Venta and frequently used rituals and religious doctrine to maintain control of its population. The city was home to Mesoamerica's first pyramid, which attracted people from around the region to participate in its religious ceremonies.

The Great Pyramid at La Venta. It is around 110 feet high and filled with an approximate 3.5 million cubic feet of earth. It is entirely man-made; it has been theorized that the Olmecs built this to represent a mountain, which they considered to be sacred, to use in their religious ceremonies. (Credit: Alfonsobouchot)

It is believed that the city was first settled in 1750 BC and gradually rose in population until the fall of San Lorenzo around 900 BC marked its regional dominance. The city of La Venta was located on Mexico's largest alluvial plane in Mexico, and its territory comprised the area between the Mezcalapa and Coatzacoalcos rivers in the modern-day Mexican state of Tabasco. The city itself was located on a two-square-mile island in a coastal swamp of the Gulf of Mexico.

The city was located in close proximity to four separate ecosystems: marshes, mangrove swamps, tropical forests, and the ocean. This gave the inhabitants a variety of flora and fauna to hunt and gather throughout the region, though agriculture increasingly began to dominate the city throughout the Middle Formative period. The inhabitants of La Venta made the animals of the floodplain a significant part of their diet and increasingly established maize farms in riparian zones of the region. The city had extensive trade networks throughout the region, as archaeologists have found evidence of small military garrisons in nearby regions that protected the city's trade.

Scholars are unsure of how much of the surrounding area was under the direct control of La Venta. It is believed that the Arroyo Pesquero settlement (20 km to the south) and Arroyo Sonso development (around 35 km to the southeast) may have been controlled by the La Venta government.

Like San Lorenzo, the city had a complex society of different occupations and socioeconomic classes. La Venta had an exceptionally segregated society, as the elite were allowed to attend ceremonies in parts of the city where the rest of the population was not. Most of the city's population lived relatively far away from the central island of the city. Much of the city's population lived in the nearby settlement of San Andres and other neighboring towns and villages.

The city itself was largely built from dirt and clay, as well as the basalt that was transported from the nearby Tuxtla Mountains. Four large basalt "colossal head" sculptures have also been found throughout La Venta; these closely resemble those found at San Lorenzo.

Known as Monument One. It was found about a hundred feet south of the Great Pyramid, and it can be seen today at Villahermosa. This particular head stands at about nine feet high, and it is believed it was created between 800 and 700 BC. (Credit: Glysiak)

Excavations

Frans Blom and Oliver La Farge first published details about the city in 1925 during an expedition sponsored by Tulane University. They originally thought they discovered a Mayan city until radiocarbon dating showed that it was an older Olmec city. Because of its location in the dense jungle, it took many years for experts to realize the different remnants of the site all belonged to one city.

Mathew Stirling and Philip Drucker led the first excavations of the site throughout the 1940s. These initial excavations were funded by the Smithsonian Institution and the National Geographic Society. Stirling's published works about his findings at La Venta greatly helped scholars understand the Olmec culture.

The National Geographic Society once again funded an expedition led by Philip Drucker, Robert Heizer, and Robert Squier in 1955 that specifically focused on the tombs and plazas of Complex A. Drucker's team discovered a multitude of artifacts, including remnants of Olmec ceramic pottery and jade jewelry. They also made some of the first maps of the city, dividing it into designated zones. The team found a total of 53 different offerings, which ranged from small tombs filled with pottery to massive underground pits filled with large serpentine blocks.

By the early 1960s, most of the city was still largely unexcavated, and many archaeologists believed that the Mexican government was not putting in adequate effort to protect the site. Illegal excavations that were not overseen by professionals, as well as the establishment of a base of operations in the city for an oil company, greatly threatened the future work of archaeologists.

Throughout the 1960s, the National Geographic Society continued funding excavations, and in 1967, it was discovered that the shape of the city mapped out by archaeologists had been completely wrong due to dense jungle foliage covering much of the area. The excavation team also took extensive carbon samples to prove that the inhabitants of the city predated Mayan civilization.

The Instituto Nacional de Antropologia e Historia conducted large excavations throughout the 1980s. These efforts mainly revolved around accurately mapping the city and creating a protective border that would help preserve the site. Since the 1980s, the La Venta site has continually been excavated and has become one of the most studied archaeological sites in the Americas, though it still faces many dangers that could inhibit further accurate excavations.

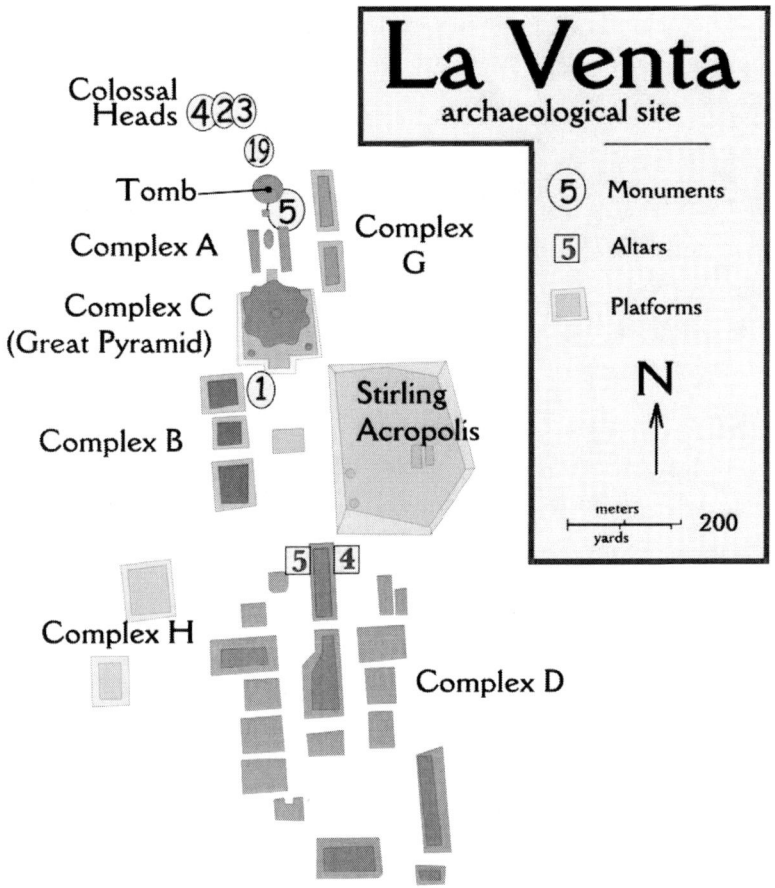

The site plan for La Venta. (Credit: Mapmaster)

In 2009, 23 different sculptures were damaged in the city by members of a Mexican evangelical church who conducted spiritual rituals that involved the pouring of saltwater, grape juice, and oil on these sculptures, including the four colossal head sculptures of the city. Following the incident, the Mexican government was pushed into enacting stricter protection laws by the Mexican population.

The Layout of the City

The central island of the city was reserved for the houses of the elite. The island also included a sacred section restricted to the ruling class, the Great Pyramid, and the plazas in the south of the island.

Numerous altars, mounds, sculptures, and tombs found by excavators at the La Venta site show that the city had a large ceremonial value to the Olmec people of the region. The center of the city served as a massive ceremonial area, with a multitude of mounds, platforms, and tombs all pointed in the same direction, eight degrees west of north. This central area has been divided by archaeologists into four distinct zones.

In the northernmost Complex A, many ceremonial mounds surround two large courts that were only used by the elite of the city. Rows of large basalt columns separated these elite plazas from the rest of the city's population.

There are also numerous tombs built for deceased rulers in this area. Many jade ornaments were found throughout these tombs, as well as mirrors made of iron ore. These items that were left throughout this area have proved to be some of the most valuable offerings of early Mesoamerican history. Unfortunately, due to the humidity of the Gulf Coast climate, only a few bones have survived the centuries. This has made it difficult to understand exactly what kind of people were buried in these tombs.

While compared to other later mounds and plazas of later Mesoamerican society, La Venta's were not especially large; however, they were exceptionally well constructed and finely detailed. The platforms, built mostly from adobe bricks, located throughout the plaza were multi-colored, largely made from dyed sands and clay.

In Complex A, five offerings of large serpentine blocks (imported into the city) were found in the tombs of deceased rulers. Large pavement mosaics were buried in many of these tombs and were decorated with multi-color clays, and some have speculated that they were used to represent spiritual imagery.

One of the unearthed mosaics; it measures around fifteen by twenty feet and consists of nearly five hundred blocks of serpentine. (Credit: Ruben Charles)

At the eastern side of the public plaza of Complex B is the Stirling Acropolis, a large platform that was used for public ceremonies and speeches. Three small mounds were also found on the western edge of Complex B.

Complex C is home to what was the tallest structure in Mesoamerica at the time of its construction. The 110 ft tall Great Pyramid located in the very center of the town was built almost entirely out of clay, and numerous tombs and altars have been found on its summit. From that summit, onlookers could survey the entire surrounding area, including the Tuxtla Mountains, where the city obtained most of its basalt from.

It is believed that many rituals and ceremonies were conducted on this summit, as mountains were considered sacred to the Olmec belief system. Today, it more resembles a large hill due to centuries of wind erosion, but it was originally built as a rectangular pyramid that had stepped terraces along its sides.

South of the pyramid was the plaza that was devoted to ceremonies for the larger general population. A large platform stood in the middle of the area, where speeches and rituals were given before large crowds.

Little is known about Complex D, which appears to have been the location for the city's governmental buildings. Twenty mounds have been found throughout this complex, and another large plaza has been found in this complex in the south of the city.

The archaeological evidence of La Venta shows that the artwork styles of the city transformed gradually from full-round sculptures that greatly resembled those in San Lorenzo to relief sculptures that began to take on a uniquely La Ventian style.

The colossal heads found in La Venta were thought to be created around the decline of San Lorenzo, which may indicate that there was considerable cross-pollination of artwork styles during this transitional period. Another sculptural style that became prevalent during this period was the depiction of figures sitting on large thrones, with many appearing to represent the city's leaders.

The sculptural styles of the city greatly reflected the Olmec belief system, as numerous depictions of sacred natural features like mountains and freshwater springs are found throughout the city. Deity figures, often depicted as animal-human hybrids, are also found extensively throughout the city.

Seven altars made of basalt rock were found throughout the city. Altars 4 and 5 were both decorated with figures that may have represented a spiritual deity or a ruler of the city. Altar 4 shows a figure that is inside a cave or the mouth of a fictional creature. Altar

5 shows a figure that is holding a deceased human-jaguar hybrid baby. While some have asserted that this is a sign of Olmec child sacrifice, others believe that it describes a creation story of some kind.

Archaeologist Matthew Stirling posing with Altar 5. (Credit: Smithsonian Institute)

Much of the details on these altars have been faded due to centuries of erosion, but they all clearly have important spiritual components. Scholars believe that these altars were actually thrones that the leaders of the city would sit on during ceremonies and rituals.

Artifacts

While Mesoamerican scholars are still unsure of the exact religious practices and beliefs of the Olmec, artifacts found throughout La Venta have provided many clues of their spiritual beliefs. Many distinct symbols have been found carved onto stones, objects, or tombs, which could point to symbols used in the Olmec religion. Many depictions of deities, often with hybrid human-animal characteristics, were also carved throughout the city.

A relief from La Venta. This is the earliest known representation of a feathered serpent; it has been dated to 1400 to 400 BC. (Credit: Audrey and George Delange)

Jade was widely considered the most sought-after object for the Mesoamerican elite. Not only was jade extremely difficult to find in the region, but it was also very difficult to shape into jewelry. Making one single jade bead would have required a highly skilled jewelry-maker to spend many hours sawing and shaping the rock. Over 3,000 jade objects were found just in Complex A.

Archaeologists have found many skeletons covered in cinnabar and buried with obsidian mirrors, which were both used to display high status in Mesoamerican culture. The prevalence of these objects throughout tombs and other burial sites throughout the focal points of the city shows the immense wealth that the elite of the city had come to enjoy. It is clear that at La Venta, the socioeconomic gap between the ruling class and the peasant class had widened greatly, and this disparity of wealth played a decisive role in La Venta's cultural and religious practices.

The Legacy of La Venta

San Lorenzo and La Venta shared many characteristics, suggesting that many influences and people may have moved from San Lorenzo to La Venta around the time of the former city's decline. Both cities had very similar styles of sculptures, ceramics, and structures, including the "colossal heads." They also met a similar fate, as the city's population began moving out of the city around 400 BC.

While San Lorenzo was the first capital of advanced Mesoamerican society, La Venta was the first truly urban Mesoamerican society. La Venta showed complexity that dwarfed any other Mesoamerican city of the time period. Perhaps most importantly, La Venta has proven to be one of the most helpful sites to archaeologists who have tried to understand the Olmec culture.

Throughout the Middle Formative period, the city of La Venta acted as much more than a population center; it acted as a cultural hub for the region that solidified its peoples' cultural beliefs and practices. During the golden age of La Venta, massive construction projects carried out throughout the city reflected the rapidly expanding sophistication of Mesoamerican society. The prevalence of sacred and luxury objects among the city's elite, as well as the way that the Olmec belief system was ingrained into the landscape of the city, shows enormous contrast to the small hunter-gatherer villages that comprised the region only a few centuries earlier.

By the end of the Middle Formative period, it was clear that Mesoamerican society was rapidly shifting into an increasingly urban, interconnected civilization that revolved around distinctive cultural practices and beliefs. However, it would soon be clear that the Olmec civilization would not survive the rapidly changing cultural climate of Mesoamerica completely intact.

While archaeologists are still largely conflicted on many parts of the cultural practices, spirituality, and day-to-day life of the Olmecs, La Venta has shed light on many aspects of the changing Mesoamerican landscape throughout the Middle Formative period. Though the city would experience a similar mysterious decline to San Lorenzo, it would forever remain the central archaeological site for Olmec culture and perhaps the final great city of the Olmec people.

Chapter 3: Olmec Decline and the Epi-Olmecs

From 400 to 350 BC, the Olmec population of the Gulf Coast cities decreased drastically. Scholars have not yet reached a consensus on why the Olmec civilization collapsed. Many believe that it was caused by changing environmental factors, which could have destroyed the livelihoods of Olmec communities that were wholly dependent on crop yields.

A change in the flow of the region's river systems may have disrupted both farming operations and trade in the region. The change of river flow may have occurred naturally or from their agricultural practices, which could have silted up the rivers. Other experts believe that the depopulation of the region was caused by volcanic activity.

Around 400 BC, as Olmec society was declining in the region, the Epi-Olmec culture began to grow in the western region of the Olmec heartland. While many distinct Olmec cultural hallmarks were lost in the rise of the Epi-Olmec, most scholars agree that this was a transformation of Olmec culture instead of a direct break from it.

Important Epi-Olmec sites. (Credit: Madman2001)

The Late Formative period that characterized the rise of the Epi-Olmec saw a large decline in trade and commerce among Mesoamerican societies. The Epi-Olmec art was also vastly inferior to the Olmec art of La Venta and San Lorenzo. The sculptures found in Epi-Olmec settlements like Tres Zapotes had much less detail and depth than traditional Olmec art, suggesting that craftsmanship took on a much less important role in their society.

While much of the great Olmec art of the Epi-Olmec's predecessors focused on depicting their rulers, artists of the Epi-Olmec focused much of their work on capturing historical events. During this period, artwork and inscriptions found throughout Epi-Olmec sites increasingly began to show a date next to it, which was practically unheard of by their predecessors.

These inscriptions largely used the Isthmian Script, the earliest writing system of Mesoamerica, dating back to 500 BC. The script has many characteristics of the Maya script that would be used centuries later. It is believed that the script originated in the Isthmus of Tehuantepec and made its way to Olmec cities through cultural diffusion and Gulf Coast trade networks.

Tres Zapotes

The greatest city of the Epi-Olmec, Tres Zapotes, was located on the western portion of the Olmec heartland in modern-day Veracruz on the western part of the Los Tuxtlas Mountain range. The city became populated around 900 BC, around the time of the decline of San Lorenzo, and reached its height of power during the 5th century BC. The city was inhabited well past the 4th century but gradually lost its power in the region.

The location of Tres Zapotes was a prime location for a thriving Olmec city, as it was surrounded by a variety of ecosystems and resources. The nearby upland forests and lowlands swamps proved to be great hunting grounds while also providing the city many natural resources like timber. The nearby mountain range also gave the city access to basalt stone that could be used to erect monuments.

Tres Zapotes also benefited greatly from the Arroyo Hueyapan River running directly through the city. During the golden era of the Olmec, the city was one of the great trading hubs for the Gulf Coast Olmec, and there is evidence that the city traded with other civilizations from northern Guatemala to Central Mexico. However, the proliferation of trade in the region would sharply decline during the Epi-Olmec era.

From 400 BC forward, the city began a transitional period from traditional Olmec to Epi-Olmec culture. While the architectural and artistic achievements of the city dwarfed that of San Lorenzo and La Venta, the Ep-Olmecs made great achievements in the Mesoamerican calendar and writing system that was growing increasingly sophisticated.

Unlike the well-connected trade routes of La Venta and San Lorenzo, Tres Zapotes was not a central hub of Mesoamerican trade networks during the Epi-Olmec era. Some experts believe that the decline in Olmec trade was caused by the cocoa plant, as many trade routes were diverted to Maya cocoa traders. The epi-Olmec also traded much less luxury elite items like jade and obsidian, indicating that the cities' elite's material wealth greatly declined, or the epi-Olmec were forced to shift their focus from the region's trade to sustenance and survival.

Structures

Over 150 structures have been found throughout the Tres Zapotes archaeological site, with most being built sometime between 400 BC and 200 AD. While Olmec cities tended to have a main central plaza or courtyard in the center of the city, the layout of Tres Zapotes was much more dispersed and spread out. Many of the site's most famous structures were found well outside the center of the city.

The dwellings of the ruling elite were also decentralized, with several royal areas spread out through the site. This may indicate that the system was ruled by several different families or factions instead of one governing body.

Two colossal giant heads have been found in the vicinity of the city's ruins, though they are much smaller than those found at San Lorenzo and La Venta. The sculptures found at the city's archaeological site highlight this transformation, as traditional religious depictions gradually turned into more secular historical depictions.

Monument A from Tres Zapotes. It stands around five feet tall and five feet wide. It weighs close to eight tons. (Credit: HJPD)

Stela C, one of Tres Zapotes' most famous structures, included an inscription of one of the city's powerful rulers depicted as a jaguar-like figure. But more importantly, the stela includes a date from the Long Count calendar. While the calendar had been gradually developing throughout the Olmec heartland, Tres Zapotes was one of the first cities where a date was inscribed on architecture. This calendar would soon become a central part of Mesoamerican life and one of the defining features of the Maya civilization.

By the mid-3rd century AD, the surrounding settlements of Cerro de las Mesas and Remojadas replaced Tres Zapotes as the dominating cities of the region. Unlike the two preceding cities,

Tres Zapotes did not see a sudden depopulation of its inhabitants. The city would remain populated up to 900 AD but would gradually leave its Olmec influences behind in its transition to Classical Veracruz culture.

The Legacy of the Olmec

While trade was already an integral part of Mesoamerican society before the rise of the Olmecs, they were the first merchants of the region to travel regularly travel across long distances to trade with other cities and civilizations. These trade routes brought great economic prosperity to the Gulf Coast cities like San Lorenzo and La Venta, but more importantly, they spread Olmec cultural influences far and wide throughout Central America. These merchants also brought back cultural ideas from other civilizations and populations to the Olmec cities. The prevalence of Olmec trade in the region caused Mesoamerica to be more closely connected and contributed to great cultural diffusion between populations.

Many of the religious beliefs of later civilizations like the Aztecs and Maya stem from the Olmec pantheon, with many worshiping the same gods as the Olmec did centuries before them. The human-jaguar figures that were found throughout Olmec cities would later become a central part of later Mesoamerican religion. The tombs and structures of many Classic Maya cities depicted their divine rulers as jaguar figures that greatly resemble the Olmec depictions.

The Olmec artists, artisans, and architects made perhaps the most impressive achievements of early Mesoamerican society. The colossal, intricately constructed structures that were found throughout the Olmec cities dwarfed anything that had been constructed in Central America before. Though some designs, such as the colossal heads, would be left in the past, the civilizations that came after the Olmec used cities like San Lorenzo as a shining example of what a powerful urban center should be.

The Olmec are credited with creating the first solidified writing system of Mesoamerica. They also made great progress in creating an accurate calendrical system and mapping the solar system. All three of these Olmec innovations would be gradually perfected and expanded upon by the Maya.

At the beginning of the 5th century BC, the Epi-Olmec emerged as a transitional civilization, expanding on the innovations and foundations of their predecessors while leaving other antiquated cultural ideas in the past. The Zapotec civilization to the south on the Pacific coast, the great city of Teotihuacan in the Valley of Mexico, and the Maya civilization of the Yucatan to the east would soon emerge as the dominating peoples of Mesoamerica.

While the Olmec would gradually fade into the distant background of the region's political order, these civilizations would continually build upon what Mesoamerica's first advanced civilization created.

Chapter 4: The Preclassic Maya Era

As Olmec society on the Gulf Coast was gradually transforming into the Classical Veracruz culture, to the east, the small settlements of the Yucatan Peninsula were increasingly growing larger. Though these small towns had many characteristics of the Olmec, they began to develop many distinct cultural characteristics of their own. As the Olmec cities of the Gulf were gradually declining, the Maya of the Yucatan were slowly becoming the greatest civilization of Central America.

The Preclassic Maya period includes the establishment of permanent settlements around the beginning of the first millennium BC up to the Classic period around 250 AD. The Preclassic period is divided into the Early Preclassic (before 1000 BC), Middle Preclassic (1000-400 BC), and Late Preclassic (400 BC-250 AD). The largest cities of the Preclassic were El Mirador, Cival, San Bartolo, Seibal, Nakbe, and Uaxactun.

In the decades leading up to the beginning of the Classic period in 250 AD, there was a "Preclassic Collapse," when many of the cities that flourished during the Preclassic period were rapidly depopulated. This would create a mass dispersal of their populations, who moved to other cities that would become the great urban centers of the Classic period.

The Yucatán Peninsula

During the Olmec golden age, Maya settlements were increasingly growing more complex throughout the Yucatan Peninsula, which would eventually become the Maya heartland. The peninsula is largely comprised of lowland plains of dense rainforest that have very few hilly or mountainous regions.

The most northern regions of the peninsula receive much less rainfall than the other regions, making the northern cities especially susceptible to drought. The ground of the northern and northwest regions in the coastal plain is largely made of limestone, and this region of the peninsula has a plethora of natural limestone cave systems created by erosion from rainfall. The region is also known for its massive sinkholes, which are created when these cave systems collapse.

The northeastern region is largely known for its vast swamplands, which served as a great defensive boundary between other regions of the peninsula. The northern coastal plain had very few river systems, with most of the peninsula's rivers being located in the southern lowlands and highlands.

The Petén Basin, located in the central lowlands, is characterized by a diverse array of topographic features, including dense rainforests, swamps, and lakes. The annual rainfall for the entire peninsula is 43 inches, with the wet season running from June to September and the dry season running from October to May. The Petén region receives the most rainfall in the peninsula, which contributed to it becoming the dominant region for the great cities of the Classic period.

Early Preclassic

Evidence has shown that agriculture existed in the Maya lowlands dating back to 3000 BC. These were most likely nomadic or sparsely populated populations that gradually created permanent villages. Hunting and gathering was the primary source of sustenance for the Preclassic Mayas, though the cultivation of maize increasingly became the dominant food source.

Ceramic pottery began to be created during this period, with many styles borrowed from the Olmecs and other neighboring Mesoamerican cultures. The Early Preclassic Mayas had a close trading relationship with the Olmecs, and immense cultural diffusion occurred between the two cultures.

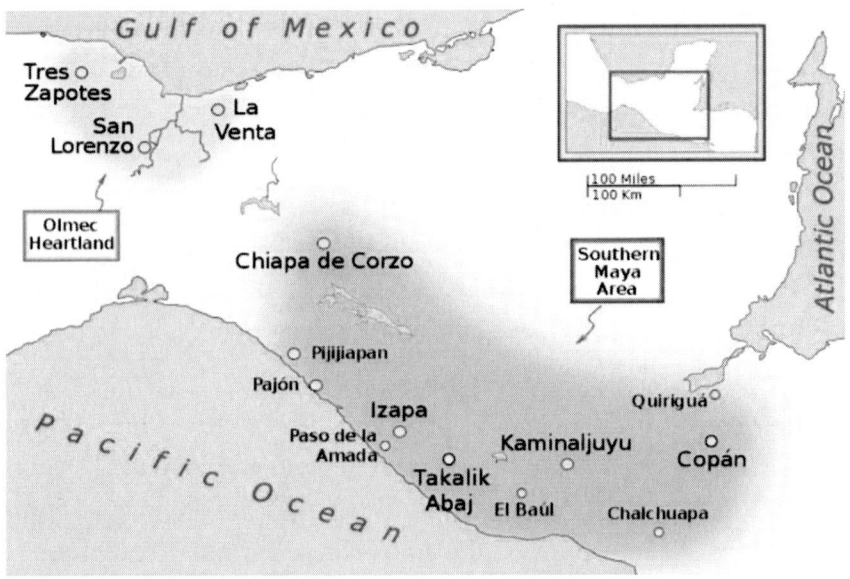

A map of the major southern Mayan cities. (Credit: Lumen Learning)

Middle Preclassic

By the beginning of the first millennium BC, the city of Aguada Fénix was a prosperous urban center in Tabasco. The construction of Aguada Fénix marked the beginning of the permanent agrarian settlements of the Maya people. Up until the city's construction, the

Maya people of the region were largely nomadic and didn't produce a significant amount of pottery.

The archaeological record points to this point in Maya history as a time when distinctive Maya ceramics were produced more frequently, and settlements became larger and more populated. This period of transformation marked the beginning of the Maya city-states that would soon dominate the region.

Trade between different regions and settlements became more frequent, and the exchange of luxury items such as jade and obsidian artifacts increased greatly. Infrastructure projects, such as canals and irrigation systems, became larger and more complex as well.

The small settlements of the Preclassic increasingly took on the organizational characteristics of large cities, such as having large plazas in their center and a vast array of ceremonial monuments and structures. Many of the architectural projects of this period borrowed heavily from the nearby Olmec cities like La Venta and San Lorenzo.

Evidence has also pointed to a rise in warfare during this period, as Maya weapons greatly improved, and kings were increasingly depicted as warriorlike figures. There have also been discoveries of mass graves that are dated to this period that show evidence of the execution of prisoners of war.

Late Preclassic

By the Late Preclassic, the city of Kaminaljuyu controlled much of the Maya highlands, while the city of El Mirador controlled the lowlands. There is evidence that the Maya of the highlands began to expand north into the southern and central lowlands during this period, where the great cities of the Classic period would soon emerge.

Many Olmec cultural practices and beliefs inspired the Maya, as their own distinctive cultural practices became increasingly complex. Throughout the Preclassic and into the Classic, the Maya people began to create a civilization that increasingly had its own characteristics that broke away from the Gulf Olmec traditions and began to create a distinctive Maya culture. By the Late Preclassic, the iconic Mayan stepped pyramids were being built in some cities, indicating that spirituality and religion increasingly became an integral part of city life.

Late Preclassic Maya sculpture found in Kaminaljuyu. (Credit: Wikimedia Commons)

Preclassic Agriculture

Many scholars have been puzzled by the population size of the Maya cities of the Preclassic and Classic periods throughout the Yucatan Peninsula. The cities of the lowlands were located in one of the most unlikely places in the world for an advanced agricultural civilization. The Yucatan Peninsula and its surrounding area were filled with dense rainforests, infertile soils, impenetrable swamplands, and severe seasonal droughts.

Just like the early Olmecs, the Maya gradually transformed from small settlements of hunter-gatherers to large settlements of agriculturalists centered around the cultivation of maize. While maize was the primary crop of the Maya people, beans, squash, and many other crops were also grown by Maya farmers.

Despite not having the advantage of metal tools and domesticated animals that the contemporary farmers of Europe had, the Maya were some of the most advanced agriculturalists of their time. The Maya largely used slash and burn agricultural techniques. This method involved cutting down a given forested area and then burning it. Crops would then be planted in the nutrient-rich ashy dirt of the burnt area. After using this burnt area several times, they would move to new land to allow the area to regenerate. This proved to be a highly effective method for the Maya, though as the Classic cities grew, it would also contribute to heavy deforestation of the lowlands.

The Maya also used complex irrigation and terracing techniques by taking advantage of the many swamps dispersed throughout the Yucatan region. Maya engineers used ingenious methods to divert water sources throughout the wetlands into canals to create more fertile arable land. In the mountainous highlands, terraces were frequently cut into the sides of mountains to grow maize.

Gender also played a major role in agricultural Maya society. While men tended the fields, hunted, and fought in battles, women were put in charge of running the home and carrying out domestic duties.

By the Classic period, Maya agriculture and water management had become extremely efficient and could support large urban populations. The surplus of crops and a large growing population that could craft luxury items like ceramics led to increased trade throughout Maya society.

El Mirador used a water collection system; above, you can see the stucco friezes that adorned it. (Credit: Geoff Gallice)

El Mirador

There is no better example of the ingenious methods used in Preclassic agriculture than El Mirador. The city of El Mirador was the great city of the Maya lowlands during the Late Preclassic. It blossomed as the central trading hub of the region from around 300 BC to the 1st century AD.

El Mirador was surrounded by a multitude of wet swamplands, which turned the city into one of the most efficient agricultural centers in the region. The farmers brought hundreds of tons of mud from the swampy areas and used it to create terraces throughout the city's farms. The pH of the soil was increased by adding lime to it, which allowed the nutrient-deplete soil of the region to grow a variety of crops.

Around the beginning of the Common Era, El Mirador and many other neighboring cities saw a massive exodus of its population as part of the "Preclassic collapse." Environmental studies have shown that the region surrounding El Mirador was heavily deforested by the time of the collapse. A large proportion of the surrounding forest was cut down to produce lime and for other architectural projects.

With the absence of trees in the region, much of the nutrient-deplete soil was no longer held down by natural vegetation and was swept into the swamplands by heavy rainfall. The nutrient-rich mud of the swamps that once served as the secret ingredient for the city's agricultural boom was gradually covered by layers of soil from the surrounding areas.

Preclassic Architecture

The timeline of Maya architecture shows the great progression of their civilization. From their roots in stone age village communities, by the Late Preclassic period, the Maya were constructing some of Mesoamerica's largest and most complex structures. The many impressive monuments and buildings of the lowland Classic cities were predominately built with limestone, while the highland cities mostly used sandstone and igneous rocks.

A photo of La Danta, a temple located in El Mirador. It stands at around 236 feet tall and is considered to be one of the largest pyramids in the world. (Credit: Dennis Jarvis)

While initially, the Maya built structures out of necessity to support their growing populations, the architecture of the lowlands increasingly began to be characterized by elements that promoted the city's political and religious order. The architecture was increasingly decorated with hieroglyphs and inscriptions of Maya gods, historical events, and powerful rulers. The ruling class used the architecture of the city to solidify their divine power by making religion an integral part of their cities.

Throughout the Classic period, the rulers of the Maya became inexorably linked with their architecture. The religious element of these structures echoed the belief that these great cities were constructed by divine rulers who were put on the throne by the gods. Sculptures, monuments, inscriptions, and sacred temples were all built depicting past rulers, stressing the divinity and historical significance of the ruling dynasty. In examples where scholars believe the population of the cities overthrew their rulers in revolution or revolt, many of these sacred structures and monuments were defaced and purposefully damaged.

Aside from the political and practical utility of these structures, they also possessed great astronomical and religious significance. Many of the great structures of the Maya urban centers were built oriented towards a cardinal direction. The north and south represented the heavens and the underworld, while the east and west were associated with the sun's rising and setting.

Great plazas were located in the center of nearly every Classic Maya city, usually surrounded by the city's pyramids and other large structures. These plazas served as places for the population to congregate and observe large ceremonies. Different parts of the cities were connected by causeways, which were wide streets that were made out of stone or wood. These streets all led to the central plaza and connected the city to outside settlements with which it had a trading or political relationship.

The Classic Maya architects borrowed many different architectural styles from throughout Mesoamerica. The style that was chosen often reflected an alliance system, trading relationship, or cultural background with another city. For example, the great Maya city of Tikal had many architectural designs that mirrored styles seen in the city of Teotihuacan in Central Mexico. The similarity of architecture reflects the close relationship between the two cities, as Teotihuacan conquered Tikal in the Early Classic period and maintained a strong cultural connection with the city throughout Tikal's political apogee.

Many cities in the Maya lowlands also had architectural styles that mirrored the Toltec city of Tullan in Central Mexico. Some evidence has shown that the Toltecs invaded some regions of the Maya heartland during the Terminal Classic and Postclassic periods. The Puuc style of architecture seen in cities like Chichen Itza had its roots in the center of the Maya Yucatan heartland. It used a repetitive geometric style that often included masked figures of the Maya gods.

An example of the Puuc style. This particular building is in Uxmal. (Credit: Tato Grasso)

Most of the Maya population lived in thatched-roof hamlets with one or two rooms, while the royal elite lived in palace complexes comprised of several rooms. The elite complexes grew extensively throughout the Classic period, and by the 9th century, many of them had their own courtyards and water supplies.

An example of a traditional Mayan house. (Credit: Wikimedia Commons)

While the everyday Maya population buried their deceased relatives in small tombs near their homes, the royalty was buried in elaborate tombs and temples. The burial practices of an elite figure depended on how powerful the ruler was. Most rulers were buried with valuable, sacred items like jade in decorated tombs located in a part of the city dedicated to the commemoration of the deceased elite. More powerful rulers had entire temples and pyramids dedicated to them, with many including a visual depiction of the ruler and their name and time of death.

The great step pyramids are often viewed today as the iconic symbol of the Classic Maya. These pyramids were largely dedicated to deceased rulers, and many rituals would be carried out at the top of the staircases in honor of the gods.

Many large structures built by the Maya, including the step pyramids, were continually built and rebuilt. As one structure began to grow obsolete, a new structure would be constructed on the outside of it. This allowed Maya rulers to construct buildings that were ostensibly completely new and possessed the former structure's solid foundation.

The Classic Maya also constructed some of the world's first advanced water management systems with massive reservoirs that collected rainwater for their cities. As the region was constantly under the threat of seasonal droughts and had very few riparian sources, the Classic Maya populations came to depend heavily on these urban reservoirs.

The urban Maya erected thousands of "stelae," slabs of rock often inscribed with historical events, religious depictions, or portraits of rulers. Many of the stelae included dates from the Maya calendars, which have greatly aided archaeologists in creating a timeline for Maya history.

Preclassic Collapse

A Preclassic collapse occurred around 100 AD, and scholars have yet to reach a consensus on the causes of the rapid depopulation of the Preclassic cities. Scientific evidence points to a series of droughts that enveloped the region during this period, which may have led to inadequate water supplies for the growing urban population. There is also evidence that many of the Preclassical cities had been heavily deforested by the first millennium AD, and their water supplies had been heavily contaminated by urban runoff.

Whatever the causes were, this collapse of the Preclassic cities paved the way for the population boom in the southern and central lowlands that would characterize the Classic period.

As the populations of Preclassic cities like El Mirador collapsed, ideas and culture dispersed throughout the Yucatan Peninsula. This dispersal of the Maya across the Yucatan created immense cultural diffusion, as the Maya began to settle into the towns that would soon become the greatest cities of Mesoamerica.

PART TWO: THE CLASSIC MAYA ERA (250-900 AD)

Chapter 5: Classic Maya Society

The Classic period of the Maya civilization was the apogee of Maya cultural, scientific, and political achievements. The cities of Tikal, Calakmul, Palenque, and Copan became the great cities of the Maya civilization. During this period, the greatest monuments and temples that define the civilization today were constructed by divine rulers who ruled over great regional political empires. The rulers of the classic period took on secular leadership and a spiritual role that proclaimed them as divine figures ordained by the gods.

The Classic period is divided into three distinct periods: During the Early Classic (250-550), the urban centers of the southern and central lowlands became the dominating cities of the Maya civilization. The Late Classic (550-830) saw these cities at their peak of population, architecture, and political power. This period saw constant warfare throughout the lowlands, as a power struggle ensued between the great cities and their alliances. The Terminal Classic (830-950) was the time of the "Classic Maya Collapse," when these cities were rapidly abandoned by their inhabitants, never to be densely populated again.

Classic Maya Political System

Unlike the Aztec civilization, which had a centralized government in its capital of Teotochtitcal, the cities of the Maya civilization acted as independent states that acted autonomously. Vast alliance systems were formed throughout the Maya heartland that linked these cities with cultural ties, military alliances, or trading partners.

More powerful cities also brought smaller vassal cities under their control, which usually paid tribute to the larger city in exchange for military protection and access to trade networks. Within the cities of the Classic period, the urban Mayan political systems revolved around hereditary rulers who believed that the gods chose them to rule their populations.

The Classic Maya had four socioeconomic levels. The kings and high royalty of the largest cities like Tikal and Calakmul were considered the highest class of Maya society. Next were the smaller vassal states' leaders, who were considered close military allies and trading partners with the larger city. Next were the village settlements that were ruled by regional nobility. Last were the hamlets located in the periphery of urban Maya society, which were solely dedicated to farming or some other small-scale production of goods.

Powerful kings in Maya cities did not become common until around the 4th century AD, when large stelae began being erected throughout urban areas that commemorated the city's royalty. The royalty considered themselves halfway between humans and gods and believed they had a sacred duty to act as an intermediary between the two.

There are examples of queens ruling cities, but this usually only happened when there was not a suitable male heir for the throne. Young men of royal families that were destined for the throne were often military leaders and led campaigns against enemy city-states.

Kings were expected to be on the battlefield and personally lead their troops into battle. The capturing of enemy royalty was one of the most important parts of Maya warfare. Captured kings or nobles were not always executed, but many were sacrificed in large ritualistic ceremonies.

Enormous, lavish palaces where the royal families resided were an inescapable part of Classic Maya urban centers. These palaces would usually be constructed in the city's central plaza near the great temples and other large structures.

Throughout the Classic period, the royalty of the Maya cities increasingly lived lavishly. The small, modest palaces of the Early Classic eventually turned into elaborate complexes by the Terminal Classic. Many scholars have pointed to revolution or an overthrow of the royal class due to rising income inequality as a possible reason for the collapse of the Classic cities. It would make sense that a population that increasingly found itself in dire circumstances would grow resentment towards a divine ruling class that lived so extravagantly right before their eyes in the center of their city.

Religion

It is impossible to visit the ruins of the Classic Maya cities today without noticing the evidence of a complex spiritual belief system. The gods of the Maya played an integral role throughout their society, from agriculture to the divine rulership of kings. The spirituality of the Maya revolved around the belief that the entire world was enveloped by "k'uh," which translates to "sacred."

Maya priests were tasked with overseeing the religious order of their society. This entailed conducting ceremonies and observing the sky to decipher the "will of the gods."

Some Maya gave the sun and moon distinct characters, with the sun being a masculine figure and the moon being feminine. They believed the gods placed the sun and moon on Earth but were brought into the heavens as punishment due to the feminine moon's infidelity.

Death was an important part of the Maya religion, especially for rulers. Entire sections of cities were solely dedicated to the burials and commemoration of deceased rulers. The Maya believed that the soul traveled to the underworlds after death, which is often depicted as a dark place ruled by jaguar-like gods.

The Maya believed that time worked cyclically instead of linearly. They believed that different worlds had existed before them, and many others would exist after them. They believed that their world would come to an abrupt ending one day, and the gods would create a new world.

While the practice of human sacrifice is certainly overblown in popular media depicting the Maya, it was practiced widely in the Classic cities. The shedding of human blood was considered a divine and necessary offering to the gods. Prisoners of war and rulers of rival cities were the most commonly sacrificed peoples.

The creation of the universe is one of the most important components of the Maya religion. In the beginning, the sky and the earth were attached to each other, and there was no room for any life to exist on the planet. The gods planted a large tree on the earth to lift up the sky and create room for the existence of life. While the tree grew, its roots stretched down to the depths of the underworld, and its branches reached up into the upper world. Animals and vegetation began to inhabit the earth, but the gods were displeased because there were no advanced beings that could use verbal communication to praise them, so they created humans.

The Maya Creation Story

The Maya believed that they were living in the third cyclical creation of the universe and that the two previous ones had been destroyed. They believed that theirs too would eventually be destroyed by the gods.

In the first creation of the universe, the people were made entirely of mud, meaning they could not move or think critically. The gods were displeased with the mud beings and destroyed the world with floods of boiling water. The gods then made humans out of wood. While they were much more productive and advanced than the mud people, they were soulless and did not praise their gods. Like the population before them, the gods destroyed them with water. The beings that were somehow able to survive these two universes were believed to be monkeys.

Modern humans were created in the third creation when the gods decided to make the beings out of dough made from maize and the blood of gods. The gods considered the four beings they created too intelligent, and they were afraid they would overthrow them and take control of the universe. The gods decided to blur their minds so they would be less divine and intelligent.

The destruction of the universe occurred when the beings no longer worshiped their gods. This made it imperative for the Maya to continually and emphatically make religious worship a central component of society.

Pantheon and Mythology

The Maya pantheon is comprised of a long list of divine deities that cover nearly every component of life for the Maya people. While many of the deities were a universal part of the religious beliefs of all the Maya people, the pantheon could change significantly based on the region. As seen below, many of these gods had similar characteristics. The dependence of the Maya on rain and agriculture for their survival made the sun, rain, and weather symbols like the lightning bolt reoccurring themes in the pantheon.

Itzamná is considered the main creator of the universe and is often portrayed as an iguana or an elderly figure. He was also the god of wisdom, writing, and knowledge. He was also considered one of the most important sun gods. His wife, Chebel Yax, is also often portrayed as an iguana-like figure. Both figures are considered as two of the highest-ranking deities of the Maya pantheon.

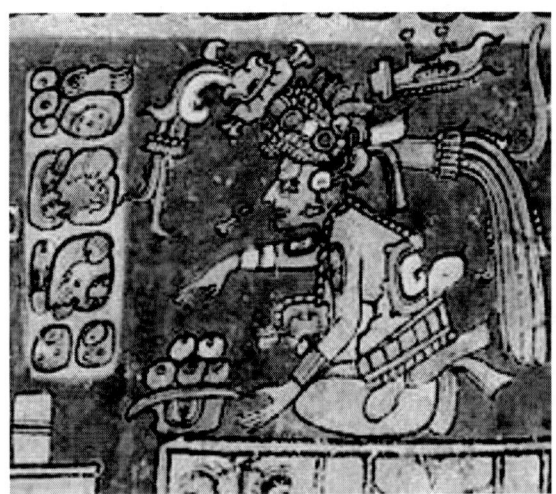

A depiction of Itzamna. (Credit: Francis Robicsek)

Huracán, the deity of the wind and sky, is also credited with being one of the universe's creators to the highland Maya. He is depicted as a one-legged god who is often holding a lightning bolt.

K'inich Ajaw was one of the most powerful sun gods of the religion. The sun gods were considered some of the most powerful and sacred gods because of the Maya's reliance on agriculture and freshwater: too little sun and their crops wouldn't grow, and too much son would bring severe droughts that would devastate the region. Every day, he was born in the east as the sun rose and aged throughout the day until the sun set in the west. After the sun disappeared beyond the horizon, he would turn into a jaguar-like figure and become a warrior in the underworld.

Hun H'unahpu is considered the most important of the deities, as he was the god of maize, the central food of Mesoamerica. He was most often depicted as a young man with long hair. The second most important god was Chak, the rain god. Chak is often depicted as a man-reptile hybrid. The Maya believed that both Chak and Hun H'unahpu required human blood.

K'awiil is most often described as the god of royalty and lightning and is depicted with a lightning bolt in his hand. Ah Puch, also called Kisim, is the god of death and is most often portrayed as a rotting skeleton figure. He is often depicted holding an owl, which was considered an intermediary messenger between Earth and the underworld.

Akan is another death god that is specifically associated with drinking and disease. Akan is often depicted vomiting and holding wine, and in some depictions, he is cutting off his own head. Ix Chel is the god of rainbows, often depicted wearing a headdress made of snakes. She represents femininity, along with childbirth and fertility, and is often depicted with images of the moon.

The Ceiba tree, a tropical tree species native to Central America, was sacred to the Maya people. The Ceiba is often cited in Maya inscriptions as the tree in the creation story that the gods planted to separate Earth from the skies. Its essential role in the creation story made it the symbol of the universe for the Maya. Inscriptions of the tree describe its roots flowing down into the underworld, while its large trunk represented Earth's existence in the middle world, and its branches reach up to the upper world. Depictions of the tree exist in the codices and many inscriptions and murals found throughout Classic Maya cities.

An example of a Ceiba tree; this picture was taken in Chiapas, Mexico. (Credit: Alejandro Linares Garcia)

The cardinal directions were important to the Maya, especially east and west, because of the sun's rising and setting. Each direction was given a different color, with north being white, east being red, south being yellow, and west being black. Particular gods were assigned these directions, and many temples, tombs, and shrines were built perfectly facing a cardinal direction because of their spiritual significance.

The Maya believe that the universe existed in three levels. The middle world is Earth, while the gods inhabit the upper world and underworld. The upper world contained thirteen levels, while the underworld was comprised of nine levels.

The underworld, called "Xibalba" by the highland K'iche and "Mitnal" by the Yucatec, was important to the Maya belief system. The underworld was ruled by an array of terrifying, bloodthirsty gods who would periodically ascend to Earth to bring death and destruction to mankind. Souls entered the underworld either through a water-filled underground cavern or through the sky and would be confronted by a hellscape of ghastly scenes and creatures.

Astronomy

It is impossible to discuss the religious beliefs of the Maya without mentioning their connection with astronomy. The Maya were some of the most advanced astronomers in the world and were able to accurately count the exact solar year of the region.

The Maya used towering observatories and temples to theorize about the solar system, which they used for secular scheduling of agricultural production and water storage. However, the study of astronomy went far beyond pragmatic scheduling and timekeeping. Astronomy played a major role in the spiritual and religious beliefs of the Maya as well.

The observatory at Chichen Itza; it is known as Caracol. (Credit: Wikimedia Commons)

They believed that when observing the night sky, they were being shown messages and revelations by their gods. The Maya believed that Earth was located in the center of the universe and that the planets and stars above were gods that were moving throughout the spiritual realm.

The sun was one of the most important aspects of Maya astronomy, and the sun god, Kinich Ahau, was one of the most important deities of their religion. The Maya believed that Kinich Ahau would travel to the underworld at night after staying in the sky throughout the daytime.

The moon also played an important role in the Maya belief system. The Maya believed that the moon goddess, Ix Chel, fought the sun god every day, forcing him to make his journey down to the underworld.

Astronomy also played a role in ruling dynasties, as many murals of the Maya displayed rulers wearing clothing that symbolize the stars and planets. The astronomer-priests of Maya cities also had tremendous power. A war could be delayed until a certain planet or star was in the right place, or a new ruler could be put in place only during certain celestial cycles.

The planet Venus played an especially significant role in the Maya belief system. Venus symbolized warfare to the Maya, and attacks and conquest would be timed with the positioning of the planet.

While the planets played a significant role in the Maya belief system, the stars had a more practical place in the Maya civilization. The positions of stars were largely used to plan and schedule agricultural production.

Many monuments throughout the Maya cities have clear connections to astrology, and many buildings throughout the cities are nearly perfectly aligned with cardinal directions. The city of Chichen Itza has one of the most famous examples of this astronomical architecture. During the equinox, the sun lights up the stairs to one of the city's largest pyramids, giving the onlooker the illusion of a snake climbing up the staircase.

A picture taken during the spring equinox of 2009. It is thought the appearance of the snake represents Kukulcan, the feathered serpent deity. (Credit: ATSZ56)

Rituals and Ceremonies

Though human sacrifice has been a defining characteristic of the Maya civilization in popular media, it was most likely less common than these depictions. The most commonly sacrificed people were prisoners of war and captured rival leaders. The most common method of sacrifice was decapitation, though heart extraction, largely influenced by the Aztecs of Central Mexico, had become a common method by the end of the Classic period.

Bloodletting was practiced much more frequently than lethal human sacrifice. It was usually practiced by the nobility, as their blood was considered sacred. The practice was important to the Maya people because the gods spilled their blood in creating the universe. The spilling of their own blood showed gratitude and proved their allegiance to the gods for the creation of the Maya people. Bloodletting was usually practiced by the nobility, usually making incisions on the tongue or genitals with stingray spines.

Topographic features of the Maya heartland were a sacred part of the Maya belief system. Elaborate ceremonies were conducted on mountaintops, in cave systems that were believed to lead to the underworld, or at sinkholes that served as places of ritual sacrifice. The Maya believed that the gods gave them their land, and these features served as sacred locations to connect with the spiritual realm. Many of these landmarks, most notably a large sinkhole in the city of Chichen Itza, would regularly be used as a pilgrimage site. Maya populations also had a number of regional shrines devoted to local saints that were journeyed to regularly.

Priests were the leaders of spiritual life in Maya society, overseeing ceremonies, sacrifices, and probably the construction of sacred temples and other religious architecture. The priests also had tremendous knowledge of other subjects, such as astronomy, timekeeping, and mathematics. The synthesis of these subjects and the traditional religious beliefs gave priests enormous power in the Maya political system. Priests would often decide the ascension of rulers to the throne or the right time to go to war based on the cycle of the planets or the religious significance of dates on the calendar.

Body Modification

Body modification was a widespread part of Maya culture. Piercings, tattoos, and the sharpening of teeth were often used for individualistic expression that displayed a person's cultural ties or their political status. These often excruciatingly painful modifications would often serve as a rite of passage for young men who aspired to be warriors or were in line to become rulers.

One of the most painful of these was cranium modification, which was a cultural practice probably handed down from the Olmec. This entailed shaping the head into a variety of shapes using an array of different devices, including special cradles that were used to compress the skull while laying down and a device made of paddles that the child could wear throughout the day. The most common shape was a tall skull with a flattened forehead, which was usually created by clamping two paddles on each side of the child's head.

A deformed female Olmec skull. (Credit: Gary Todd)

By the time of the 10th century, this practice had become widespread throughout the population of Maya cities, though citizens belonging to the lower classes normally had less obvious modifications. In many cities, the members of elite families were forced to go through some form of cranium modification. This process usually began when the children were toddlers, a time when the skull is still in the growing process and more malleable than a fully formed adult skull.

Dental modification was also widely practiced throughout Maya society. Many Maya warriors sharpened their teeth to intimidate enemies, while many noblewomen had precious stones like jade drilled into their teeth.

Body paint was an important Maya cultural practice and would be specially used during ceremonies. Priests would often color themselves red using cinnabar during religious occasions, and sacrificial victims were often painted before their blood was spilled for the gods. Tattoos were a sign of great bravery for Maya men, as it was an extremely painful process. Most tattoos were simply cut into the body with obsidian weapons. Piercings were common among Maya populations, as jewelry made from precious stones was a marker of high status or beauty.

Writing System

Many components of the Maya hieroglyphic system were passed down from their Olmec predecessors. Maya hieroglyphs and inscriptions became common throughout Yucatan settlements by 300 BC, and by the beginning of the Classic period, the Maya writing system was an integral part of the architecture of the region's urban centers. Stelae, temples, and tombs were covered in inscriptions giving descriptions of historical events, mythology, or the names of rulers.

The script used by the Maya combined symbols and images that denote certain objects or actions with symbols that represented pronunciations of the spoken language. While it is not fully known how much of the urban Maya populations were literate, the full comprehension of the writing system was most likely only taught to the elite, as reading and writing were considered sacred abilities given by the gods.

The Codices

The Maya took scrupulous notes on their history, astronomical observations, and their belief system, but nearly all of these records were destroyed by the Spanish missionaries of the 16th century. These missionaries destroyed these records to erase both the native religion of the Maya and their pre-Colombian history. Four of these extensive historical records, called the "codices," survived the evangelization efforts of the missionaries and have been a tremendously helpful tool for understanding the Maya civilization.

The most important of these codices is the Dresden Codex. It is considered one of the oldest and best-preserved books written by Mesoamericans, despite heavy water damage inflicted on it by the allied bombing of Dresden during World War II. The discovery of the Dresden Codex showed historians and archaeologists the great extent of Maya astronomical knowledge. The Madrid Codex explains many of the religious beliefs of the Maya and many parts of everyday Mesoamerican life. The Paris Codex solely covers the rituals and ceremonies of the Maya. The Grolier Codex, located today in Mexico City, is the only codex whose authenticity is under question.

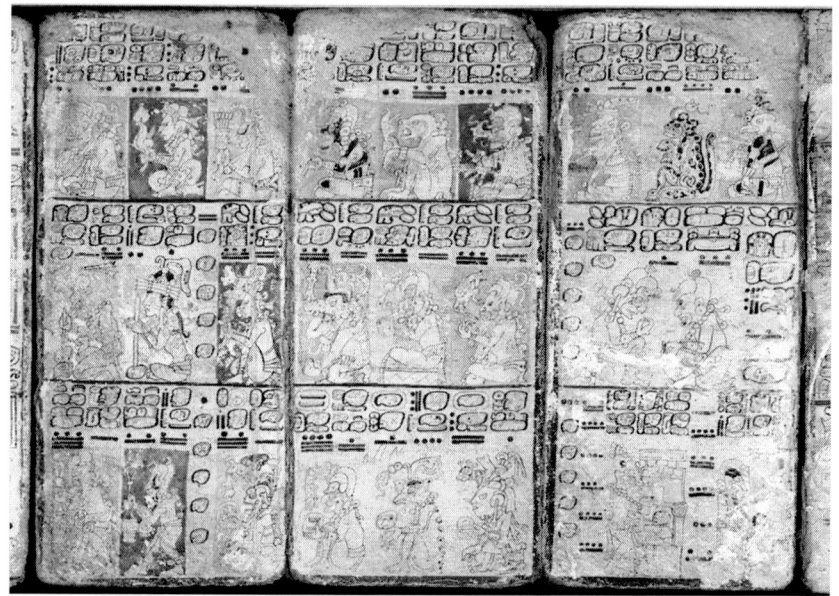

Pages from the Dresden Codex. (Credit: Wikimedia Commons)

Popol Vuh and Chilam Balam

The Popol Vuh, which translates to "The Book of the People" in the Mayan language, is one of the most sacred books of the Maya people. It was written by the K'iche' Maya of the Guatemalan Highlands, mainly focusing on the highland Maya religion. It also goes into detail about the settlement of the highlands by the K'iche' people. The book is considered so sacred because Spanish priests destroyed most Maya texts during the 16th and 17th centuries.

A Maya scribe wrote the Popol Vuh during the 16th century, and it became a cherished text of the highland K'iche' people. When the Spanish conquered the region, the Maya were able to keep it hidden until a trusted Spanish priest that was beloved by the local population was allowed to see it. Knowing that it was an important historical and cultural artifact of the local Maya, the priest translated it into Spanish.

Along with the religion's creation story, which greatly resembles the creation story of the lowland Maya, the Popol Vuh includes one of the most important chronicles of the Maya religion: the story of the Hero Twins.

The Chilam Balam is also one of the sacred texts of the Maya. The series of texts date back to the 18th century and display the breadth of lowland Maya culture, religion, and daily life. The writer of the texts created a great historical timeline, describing the migration patterns and ruling dynasties of the lowland Maya. Many riddles and poems were written in the texts and a collection of prophecies made by Maya priests.

Dance and Music

Music was a central part of Classic Maya society. Though there is no evidence of stringed instruments being used by the Maya, wind and percussion instruments were widely used during both secular and religious occasions. Primitive trumpet-like instruments were made of clay and wood, and many flutes were found in Maya cites. Drums and rattles were the main percussion instruments of Maya music and were a common household item in many regions.

Music was used by Maya populations while preparing for battle, performing rituals, or during celebrations, such as weddings. Many musical and dance traditions have survived and are performed by many modern Maya peoples throughout Central America today.

Cacao

Cacao was an integral part of the Olmec diet and their trade, but the Maya truly made the crop an essential part of their culture. Along with maize, the cacao plant was considered one of the most divine crops of the Maya heartland. According to the Maya religion, the plant was given to the people of the religion on a mountaintop by the gods.

The plant was largely drunken by the royal elite, who most often consumed it in its liquid form, which probably greatly resembled modern "hot cocoa." Cacao beans were also used widely as currency throughout the Mesoamerican trade systems. The plant was used as a medicine for many illnesses, and cacao beans would often be buried with loved ones to be used during their voyage through the underworld.

Mathematics

The Maya mathematicians were some of the most advanced in all of the Americas. Three symbols were used to count: number one was represented by a small dot, number five was represented by a bar, and a shell was used to represent zero. The use of zero is especially impressive, as very few civilizations in the world used it in their numerical system.

These numbers were used for a variety of reasons. Basic math was needed for commerce and the exchange of goods. Symbols were used because it was so easy for Maya populations to use them in their everyday lives. It was also used for more important reasons, such as making predictions based on the calendrical system.

Calendars

The Maya were fascinated with time, and timekeeping was inexorable with both their studies of astronomy and their religious beliefs.

Scholars believe that the first calendar of Mesoamerica dates back to 1500 BC, and the Maya increasingly perfected it throughout the Preclassic and Classic periods. The Maya had several calendars that were widely used throughout the Classic period, with the Calendar Round and Long Count being the most prominent.

The Calendar Round was largely used to document the holy days for religious rituals and ceremonies. This calendar used a 260-day cycle that included twenty thirteen-day periods. The Haab used a 365-day solar year that is divided into eighteen months with twenty days and one extra five-day month. The Maya inscribed pictures to each month, as they believed every month in the calendar possessed its own distinct "personality."

The Long Count Calendar, also called the "universal cycle," was used for longer periods. This calendar had strong ties to the Maya religion and the belief that the world was constantly destroyed and rebuilt by the gods. Each Long Count cycle was 2,880,000 days long, with each new cycle bringing a complete rebirth of the universe. These calendrical cycles would match every 52 years, which would mark the beginning of a new Maya century.

The calendrical system that the Maya created was an essential part of their urban society. The calendar was used to calculate when to plant crops, when to anticipate the wet or dry season, and the best time to conduct warfare. The calendar was calculated by the positioning of the stars and planets, which they believed were signs from the gods. Priests used the calendar to document both holy days for celebrations and "unlucky days," when sacrifices would have to be made to appease the gods.

These calendars have also been an indispensable tool for historians and archaeologists, as many central events were painted and encrypted with dates from the Maya calendars.

The Maya calendar gained international attention in the year 2012, as the Long Count calendar reached the end of its cycle on December 21st. While popular media increasingly speculated that this was an apocalyptic doomsday prophesy, the date was simply the end of the Maya calendar year.

Classic Maya Warfare

For many years, Mesoamerican scholars believed that the Maya were an exceptionally peaceful civilization. They proposed that the Classic period was a period of great peace throughout the Maya lowlands, as the city's prospered as their culture and art flourished.

However, modern knowledge of the Maya has completely flipped this view of the civilization on its head. The fractured state of the Maya heartland meant that cities were constantly competing for resources and political control of the region.

The seasonal droughts of the lowlands, the small number of freshwater sources, and the general infertility of the Yucatan soil made land and water the most sought-after resources for the Classic Maya. As the population of the urban cities grew, these resources became both more in-demand and scarce, leading to a massive spike in regional rivalries and warfare.

Larger cities had well-trained armies that proved to be some of Mesoamerica's most formidable military forces. These armies often made long, perilous journeys that spanned for hundreds of miles through the dense rainforest. The main weapons of the Maya were swords, spears, and bow-and-arrows, with most of these weapons being made of obsidian. The taking of prisoners was a central component of Maya warfare, especially the capture of royalty. These prisoners would often be the prime victims when human sacrifices were performed.

By the end of the Classic period, many war-torn central and southern lowlands leaders had built massive defensive fortifications around their cities. There is also evidence that the rural populations that once lived carefree on the periphery of the urban cities gradually moved inwards closer to the city. This shows that destructive warfare had become a real existential threat for many Maya populations by this time. Over the next three chapters, we will explore how warfare and many other factors led to the downfall of the Classic Maya urban centers.

Chapter 6: Tikal: The Maya Jaguar God City

Tikal was one of the Maya civilization's largest cities of the Classic period. It was located in modern-day northern Guatemala in the Petén Basin, 40 miles southwest of the modern towns of Flores and Santa Elena and 188 miles north of Guatemala City.

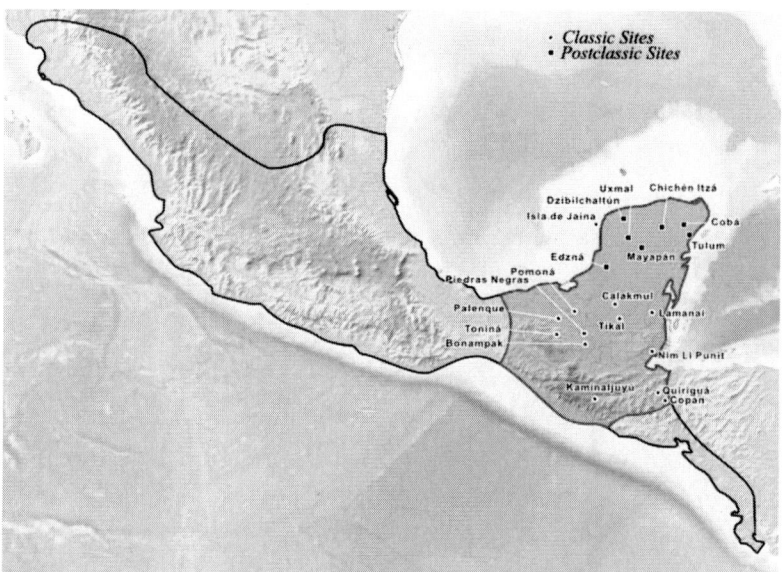

Tikal is located in the middle of the highlighted area. (Credit: Kmusser)

The city has been one of the most studied Mesoamerican sites due to its expansive documentation of rulers and its many temples, tombs, and monuments. The archaeological site became part of the Tikal National Park in 1955, making it the first federally protected area in the country. It was officially classified as a UNESCO World Heritage Site in 1979.

The city's total area was over 6.2 square miles, with around 3,000 structures being found throughout the site. Some of Tikal's oldest architecture dates back to the 4th century BC, and evidence of agricultural production in the city dates back to 1000 BC.

A collection of Maya ceramics that dated back to 700-400 BC were discovered throughout the archaeological site, indicating the presence of a permanent, urbanized population characterized by distinctive Maya cultural influences. Many of the initial major construction projects for the city took place from 400 to 300 BC, a period when Tikal was much smaller than the nearby northern cities of El Mirador and Nakbe. The dynasty of rulers of the city began in the 1st century AD and included more than 33 rulers throughout 800 years of dynastic rule.

The city enjoyed its height of regional dominance from 200 to 900 AD. Tikal dominated the Maya lowlands throughout its peak of power. Scholars have not reached a consensus on the population figures for the city, with estimates ranging from 10,000 to 90,000. From 700 to 830 AD, the city saw a massive increase in its population, but this rapidly decreased during the 9th century. The city was nearly completely abandoned by the beginning of the 11th century.

The city was located on some of the region's most fertile soils and had expansive trade networks extending throughout Mesoamerica. However, the city had no freshwater sources located in its immediate proximity, which made it very vulnerable to droughts that were brought on with the unpredictable rainfall of the region.

The city used ten large reservoirs that were used to collect rainwater in an intricate water management system that helped the city survive through dry seasons. The city's engineers built large, sloped surfaces with canals surrounding these reservoirs that were designed to catch as much rainwater as possible.

Structures

The city's most famous area is the Great Plaza, which includes an array of palaces, altars, and two of the Maya's largest pyramids facing each other on either side of the plaza. Several causeways made of limestone were built to connect the different sections of the city, acting as streets for the population and could also serve as dams during the wet season.

A recent picture of Tikal's plaza. (Credit: Bjørn Christian Tørrissen)

The 154-feet-tall Temple I, also known as the "Temple of the Great Jaguar," was built in the 730s to commemorate the death of the ruler Jasaw Chan K'awil, who led the city in its victory against the rival city of Calakmul. Temple II, the "Temple of the Mask," towers at 125 feet tall and is believed to have been constructed by Kasaw Chan K'awil in honor of his deceased wife.

On the periphery of the Great Plaza is Tikal's tallest pyramid, the Temple of the Double Serpent, towering at 230 feet tall. It is believed that the temple was built in honor of the son of Jasaw Chan K'awiil in 740. Along with these three pyramids located in the very center of the city, five other pyramids have been found throughout the archaeological site that were built for a deceased ruler.

The North Acropolis is to the north of the Great Plaza, which includes two and a half acres of sacred tombs and temples. The Acropolis has been one of the most studied archaeological sites of Mesoamerica. Construction of the North Acropolis began during the mid-4th century BC and became the central location for the burial of deceased rulers.

A view of the North Acropolis from the plaza. (Credit: Elelicht)

To the south of the plaza is the Central Acropolis, which was home to the main royal place for the ruling elite. During the early years of the Classic period, the palace was a modest ceremonial building, but as Tikal gradually became a powerful Maya city, the palace was improved to reflect the city's growing political power in the lowlands.

The Mundo Perdido is a large 650,000 square foot plaza home to the Lost World Pyramid, one of the city's premier attractions. The plaza has a special significance for the city's history, as it was the first large plaza to be constructed during the Preclassic period and ultimately the last plaza to be abandoned after the city's decline.

The restored western side of the Lost World Pyramid. It was rebuilt many times by the Maya; the first phase dates to the end of the Middle Preclassic, and the last phase dates to around 300 AD. (Credit: Simon Burchell)

By the time of the city's decline, the palace had become a massive complex with multiple buildings, courtyards, and even its own water reservoir. The city also had seven ball courts, used for a Mesoamerican ball game that was played by the population.

Early Classic Tikal

The Classic period brought a period of divine rulership to the Maya cities. Rulers were increasingly seen as divine figures that were put on the throne by the gods' will. Monuments and temples were increasingly constructed in their honor, which has helped archaeologists map out the timeline of the city's rulers.

The Tikal dynasty was created by Yax Ehb Xook in the 1st century AD, and there would be 33 rulers of the city by the 10th century. There is evidence that in 317 AD, a queen named Lady

Unen Bahlam ruled the city, ending centuries of an exclusively male dynasty.

Throughout the Early Classic period, the cities of Tikal and Calakmul became the dominating powers of the Maya heartland. As Tikal grew, it increasingly facilitated trade with its neighbors, which helped other cities in the region grow as well. However, this new power dynamic in the Maya heartland also made Takal many enemies. The Maya states of Uaxactun, Caracol, Naranjo, and Calakmul would all engage in conflict with Tikal throughout the Classic period.

During the Early Classic period, Tikal actively fought against the city of Uaxactun in numerous battles. The rival state of Caracol defeated Tikal during the Early Classic period, and Caracol took Tikal's place as the dominating power of the Maya lowlands for some time until Tikal remerged as the most powerful city in the region.

Relationship with Teotihuacan

Teotihuacan, a large city tucked into the Valley of Mexico, had a close relationship with Tikal. By the beginning of the 3rd century AD, the city of Teotihuacan had multiple embassies built in Tikal, despite being over 800 miles away. Many of Tikal's monuments and buildings built during this period had direct influences from Teotihuacan, the greatest city of Mesoamerica at the time. There is also evidence that the two populations even practiced the same religion and worshiped many of the same gods.

Tikal's fourteenth king, Chak Tok Ich'aak, constructed a grand palace that would serve as one of the city's most important structures for centuries. Evidence points to an overthrow of Chak Tok Ich'aak by the king of Teotihuacan, Siyah K'ak, in the late 4th century AD. It is also believed that this invasion was conducted with the help of some political factions within Tikal.

Upon capturing the city, Chak Tok Ich'aak was executed, and Siyah K'ak's son, Yax Nuun Ayiin I, was named ruler of the city and ruled for 47 years. Tikal would soon gain complete autonomy from the city's political power, as Teotihuacan began to decline in the 6th century. However, as Tikal rose to prominence, the cities would remain both military allies and great trading partners.

Rivalry with Calakmul

During the 6th century, the cities of Tikal and Calakmul became rival regional powers, with both forming alliances with nearby cities. Over the next centuries leading up to the Terminal period, a Maya "cold war" ensued between the two cities as each vied for political influence in the lowlands.

Calakmul quickly shifted the scale of power in its favor by establishing an alliance system with many cities throughout the lowlands, including El Zotz, El Peru, and Caracol. The alliance successfully defeated Tikal in 562 AD. While the battle did not completely destroy Tikal, its regional dominance rapidly declined for several decades. This defeat sparked a period that has been called the "Tikal hiatus," a period when no large construction projects or writing took place in the city. In the late 6th century, many of the city's monuments and structures were defaced.

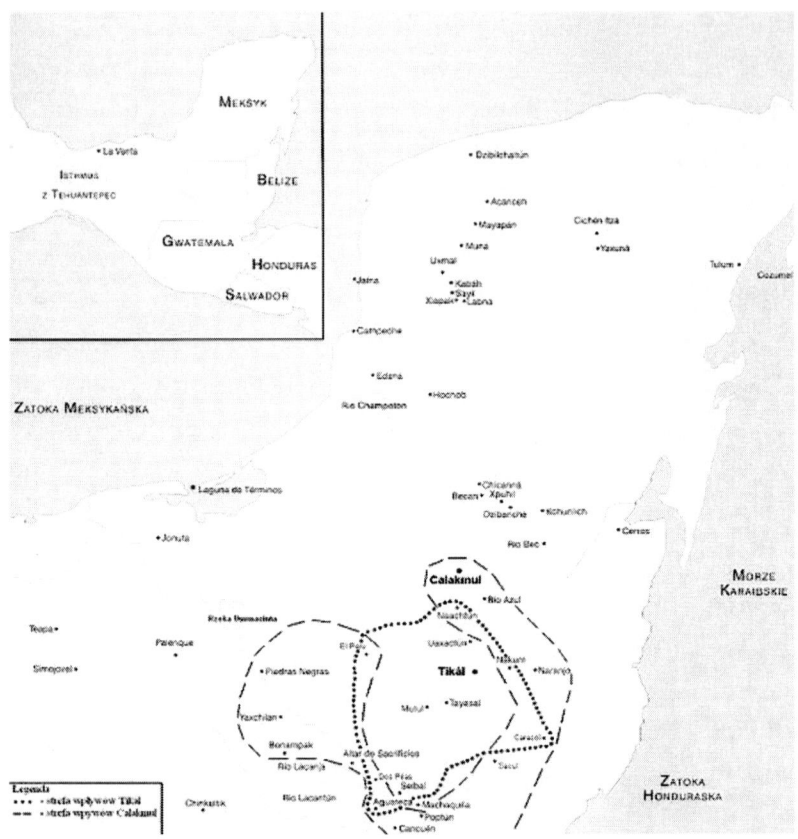

A map of Tikal's and Calakmul's allies and zone of influence. (Credit: Wikimedia Commons)

Caracol and Calakmul rose to prominence as the two most prosperous cities of the region during the Tikal hiatus. Tikal's defeat marked the end of the Early Classic and the beginning of the Late Classic Maya period.

However, Tikal slowly began to regain its strength and once again emerged as the main rival of Calakmul and its allies. Tikal created the settlement of Dos Pilas 68 miles southwest of the city in 629. Dos Pilas served as a defensive military outpost that protected the city's trade interests near the Pasion River.

In 655, Calakmul successfully invaded Dos Pilas, and the king of the city was forced to become a vassal ruler to Calakmul. With significant aid and guidance from Calakmul, Dos Pilas soon declared war on its former ruling city. Dos Pilas successfully attacked Tikal in 657, forcing Tikal's royalty to escape the city. In 672, Tikal attacked Dos Pilas in retaliation, forcing the city's rulers to flee into exile.

In 738, Tikal won a decisive victory in a head-on battle with its rival and executed the king of Calakmul. This defeat destroyed both the military and political strength of Calakmul, and the city rapidly declined. Though Tikal ultimately won the war against Calakmul, it would soon meet the same fate as its rival during the Terminal Classic period.

Settlements and Colonies

Tikal conquered a small settlement northeast of the city named Rio Azul during the late 4th century. An inscription dated to 385 found in Rio Azul depicts the city's ruling elite being executed by warriors of Tikal.

Rio Azul became closely linked to Tikal, both as a defensive garrison to protect from northern invasions and also served as a trading outpost to Caribbean trade routes. The small city also aided Tikal in its war with Calakmul due to its location on the Hondo River, which connected Calakmul to the Atlantic.

The city of Uaxactun and many other smaller Maya settlements like Bejucal and Motul de San José in the region were eventually brought under the control of Tikal. By the mid-5th century, the city controlled sixteen square miles.

Aside from these settlements that were used as military garrisons and strongholds, Tikal had many natural defensive barriers, including swamps both to the east and west of the city. During the 5th century, a massive 46 square defensive fortification system was constructed to protect the city, which indicates that warfare was growing increasingly common throughout the southern and central lowlands.

Relationship with Copan

By the 5th century, the southern city of Copan became under the control of Tikal, as the city began to spread its influence throughout southeastern Maya territory. There is evidence that the founder of the dynasty of Copan, K'inich Yax K'uk Mo', grew up in Tikal and may have been put in charge of the city by Tikal's intervention. After that, the city became one of Tikal's closest allies, both as a trading partner and a military ally.

A vassal state of Copan, Quiriguá, rebelled against its ruler in 738 and won its independence. Some experts believe that this move towards independence was aided by Calakmul, as diminishing Copan's political power would have greatly weakened Tikal's alliance system.

Terminal Classic Period

The 9th century marked a steep period of decline for the city and much of the rest of the Maya cities in the lowlands. As warfare increasingly engulfed the region, Tikal's inhabitants increasingly moved closer inwards to be protected by the city's defenses. Trade routes that connected the city with the rest of Mesoamerica were severely disrupted, and the costs of warfare drained both the city's economy and its population's morale.

Many experts believe that the fall of Tikal was caused partially by overcrowded land that caused immense environmental degradation for the area, leading to a collapse of agricultural production. The agricultural practices of the city caused massive environmental degradation in the area, as the land became over-farmed and overpopulated. The surrounding area was heavily deforested, and the soil had been depleted of its nutrients, making cultivating crops during a severe drought impossible. As a severe seasonal drought enveloped the area, these environmental problems were greatly exacerbated.

High amounts of toxic chemicals like mercury and phosphate also contaminated much of the city's water sources. Recent scholarship has indicated that the complex water management system created by the city's engineers may have contributed to the city's downfall.

The widespread use of cinnabar dye, which contains high amounts of mercury, would have resulted in a high runoff of the toxic substance into the water sources during heavy rains. Cinnabar was an escapable part of Classic Maya cities, as it was used to paint the exterior of buildings and as a dye for clothing. Also, large amounts of phosphate were found in these reservoirs, causing a blooming of toxic algae. The reservoir that was the most polluted was found near the royal palace of the city, meaning that the rulers may have been the most affected by the toxic water supplies.

By the 9th century, the reservoirs that the city's population relied on for centuries were heavily polluted. This proved to be horrific timing, as the region would experience a series of severe droughts throughout the final years of the Classic period. With no water supplies left in the city and no rainwater to collect, the population had no choice but to leave the city.

Water is an integral part of any civilization, but it was especially important in the spiritual beliefs of the Classic Maya. The pollution of their only water sources and the lack of natural rainfall may have also brought a divine spiritual element to the decline of Tikal, as much of the city's population may have believed that the city had been cursed or punished by the gods.

Between 830 and 950, Tikal's government rapidly collapsed, and much of its population left the city. Throughout the 9th-century, neighboring vassal settlements began to erect monuments that celebrated their own local rulers and customs, indicating that they used Tikal's decline as an opportunity for their independence.

Some monuments were erected in the late 9th century in an attempt to rejuvenate the city but to no avail. By the beginning of the 11th century, the city had become almost completely abandoned, with the remaining inhabitants living spread out among the city's ruins.

During the early 16th century, Spanish conquistador Hernan Cortes and his expeditionary force unknowingly passed right by Tikal and the abandoned ruins of what was only centuries before one of the greatest cities of the Maya civilization. Tikal's collapse marked a definitive moment for the Maya people. One of the region's largest cities that showcased the pinnacle of Maya art, architecture, and culture was swallowed up by the forest, never to be populated again.

Chapter 7: Calakmul: The Lost Maya Empire

Calakmul was one of the most prominent cities of the lowlands during the Classic period and proved to be the greatest rival of Tikal. The site is today located in the state of Campeche in Mexico, 22 miles from the Mexican-Guatemalan border.

Calakmul was the leading city of the "Snake Kingdom," which ruled over much of the central lowlands for the majority of the Classic period. At its height, the city was inhabited by an estimated 50,000 people, and the total area of the city spanned 7.7 square miles. Calakmul rises 115 feet above sea level with a large swampy area located to its immediate west. Its location gave the city's population access to the especially fertile soils of the swampy regions, making it one of the most productive agricultural regions of the central lowlands.

At its peak of regional dominance, the kingdom controlled 5,000 square miles of territory. The city controlled 20 settlements throughout its territory, with the combined population of these settlements being 200,000. Combining these settlements, rural areas, and the city itself, the total population of the city's kingdom was an estimated 1.5 million people during the Classic period.

However, just like Tikal, during the 9th century, the city's population plummeted rapidly to 10% of what it was only a few decades before.

There have been 6,750 structures discovered throughout the city's archaeological site, and despite its remote location away from any modern settlements, it has been one of the most excavated sites of the Yucatan Peninsula.

The Layout of the City

The primary material used to construct the many stone structures of the city was soft limestone, which is especially susceptible to erosion. The use of this material and the city's especially remote location in the dense central lowland rainforest has presented many challenges for archaeology teams in their studies of the city.

The site is a shining example of the complexity of the Maya water management systems, as large canals and reservoirs are dispersed throughout the city. The city is home to the largest reservoir of the entire Classic Maya civilization, with a surface area of 540,000 square feet. The water in this colossal reservoir was collected from a small stream that flowed into it during the wet seasons. The Calakmul region receives much less rainfall than the rest of the central and southern lowlands, so this water management system was crucial to the survival and prosperity of the city.

The 13 different reservoirs found throughout the city could hold a combined 44,000,000 gallons of water, which could potentially support a population of 100,000 people. These reservoir systems were probably solely used for consumption by the city's population, as there is no evidence of them being used in an agricultural capacity.

The city had eight different large causeways that ran through it. These causeways connected the city's periphery to its center and connected the city to its neighboring allied cities, such as El Mirador and Nakbe. The longest of these causeways, which linked the city to its close ally (El Mirador), stretched 24 miles.

Structures 1 and 2 are the main pyramids of Calakmul, located in the very center of the city. Structure 1 is 160 feet tall and has a group of small stelae erected at its base. Structure 2 is one of the largest structures of the Maya civilization, towering at 148 feet tall. Like many other Classic pyramids, Structure 2 has multiple other temples inside of it, with each structure built on top of the other.

A photo of Structure 2. Like other Mayan pyramids, Structure 2 reached its massive size over years of building upon the original foundation. (Credit: Ant_mela)

A tomb found in Structure 2 was one of the wealthiest tombs found in the Maya world, filled with many valuable artifacts made of jade, obsidian, and many ceramic crafts. It is believed that the tomb belonged to a powerful king who rose to power during the 7th century.

Structure 7 is a 79-foot-high pyramid located on the northern section of the plaza. At the very top of the pyramid is a small three-room temple that was found with a patolli game board in it. Patolli was one of the most common board games of the Maya and was played both by the city's population and their rulers. The game was often played with heavy gambling and largely revolved around luck.

One hundred and seventeen stelae have been found throughout the city's ruins, the largest number of any Classic Maya city. Most of these depicted rulers of the royal Calakmul dynasty and their wives. Like many other structures throughout Calakmul, the inscriptions have been heavily eroded due to the soft limestone composition.

The Classic Maya Marketplace

Many expansive murals were painted throughout Calakmul that depicted ordinary life in the city. Large scenes of a busy marketplace depict the bustling, populous metropolis and the everyday interactions of the Classic Maya citizenry. This is different from many other Classic cities, whose murals focus on their divine rulers, the Maya deities, or epic battle scenes.

Throughout the Classic period, urban centers like Calakmul had large, lively marketplaces that served as the economic powerhouses of the cities. These markets were usually located in the central plaza of the cities and served as a place of congregation for the city's population as they conducted their daily errands and activities. Merchants traveled throughout the Maya area and beyond, selling regional luxury items made in the city and buying exotic items from cities throughout Mesoamerica.

Most merchants of the urban centers sold their goods within the confines of the city, most likely traveling to the rural outskirts of the region to buy goods from agriculturalists and other producers. While those who traveled outside the city for trade were most likely exclusively male, both men and women could be sellers in the marketplace.

At Calakmul, the long-stretching causeways that led to other neighboring cities were most likely used by both sellers and buyers daily. It is well documented that Calakmul maintained a great trading relationship throughout the entirety of the Classic period.

The traveling merchants, called the "polom," traveled long distances to trade with other cities, with some even making frequent journeys to Central Mexico. These merchants were most often from the lower socioeconomic classes of the city, as merchants didn't have the high-class status like the long-distance traders of other Mesoamerican societies like the Aztecs.

Workshops were an essential part of Maya cities, as they made ceramics, jewelry, and other artisanal goods that were unique to the city. These cultural objects and their distinctive styles became hallmarks of the city and were sold across Mesoamerica. Cities that had close alliances, such as El Mirador and Calakmul, tended to have a considerable cross-diffusion of artisanal cultural goods.

A ceramic plate found in Calakmul, dated to 600-800 AD. (Credit: Sailko)

In the rural areas in the periphery of the cities, farmers often traded crops and goods with neighbors. When farmers had a surplus of crops during a good season, they often brought them into the marketplace to sell to the urban population. It appears that everyday sellers had great power within the cities' economies, though it is likely that the ruling class placed a tax on transactions within the city.

Early History

The cities of Calakmul and El Mirador were both prominent cities during the Preclassic period, and evidence indicates that they had a very close trading relationship. Calakmul eventually far surpassed El Mirador during the Classic period, and it is believed that many of the inhabitants of El Mirador relocated to Calakmul during the Late Preclassic. The cities of Calakmul, El Mirador, Nakbe, and El Tintal were all connected by a network of causeways, suggesting that the population could freely travel between cities.

Rivalry with Tikal

During the mid-6th century, the city began creating an alliance with many cities throughout the lowlands, and a war broke out with Tikal. The two cities became the "superpowers" of the lowlands, as each city created alliance systems and fought proxy wars to diminish the other's political power. Most scholars agree that this rivalry was most likely over control of the resources and trade routes of the region rather than an ideological war.

While Tikal had a much larger population, the leaders of Camakal proved to be shrewd diplomats that formed an alliance with the majority of the cities and settlements throughout the region. Throughout the 6th and 7th century Tikal was completely surrounded by the alliance system of Calakmul. Tikal found itself completely cut off from the rest of the lowlands, and most of its allies had either been defeated or sided with Calakmul.

During this period, Calakmul had nearly undisputed political control of the entire region, and its vast alliance system formed many new trade networks that brought the city great wealth. Many of the conquered cities throughout the region were classified as vassal states that were forced to pay tribute to Cara Kamal.

After Calakmul defeated Tikal in battle during the early 7th century, Tikal went into a rapid decline, making Calakmul the region's dominating city and ushered in the Late Classic period.

However, Tikal soon bounced back and defeated Calakmul in a great battle in 695. The king of Calakmul was killed in battle, and the city's political power sharply declined into the Terminal Classic period.

War with Palenque and Naranjo

In 599, Calakmul and the small town of Santa Elena attacked Palenque and sacked the city. After the defeat, Palenque was forced to become a vassal city and pay tribute to Calakmul. However, after only a decade after the battle, the city began to make moves towards independence, which angered the ruler of Calakmul.

In 611, Calakmul attacked Palenque, and many of the city's nobles were killed. The city was sacked by the Calakmul forces and went into a rapid decline from which it never recovered during the Classic period. It is believed that the rulers of Calakmul had a great political interest in taking the region of Palenque. They were afraid that the city would eventually ally with Tikal, and it could serve as an outpost for some of the greatest trade routes of the lowlands.

Sometime during the 620s, the nearby city of Naranjo, which had become a vassal state, rebelled against Calakmul. After some failed attempts, the city was eventually retaken in 631. The king of Naranjo was taken as a prisoner by the Calakmul warriors, and inscriptions indicate that he was tortured and executed. Inscriptions from Calakmul suggest that not only was the king executed after the battle but the entire royal family was killed. Calakmul then instated a new royal family that was firmly loyal to its political authority.

Relationship with Dos Pilas

Dos Pilas was a small settlement established by Tikal in 629 that was used to protect its trade routes on the Pasión River. The brother of the king of Tikal was named king of Dos Pilas in 635 and would fight with Tikal against Calakmul for many years.

In 648, Dos Pilas was attacked by Calakmul, resulting in the capture of the king of the city and the death of a noble elite from Tikal. Instead of executing the king of Dos Pilas, Calakmul decided instead to put him on his former throne as a vassal king to fight against his former ally, Tikal.

In 657, Dos Pilas, now with the aid and guidance of Calakmul, attacked Tikal and forced much of the ruling class to flee the city. Despite the two formerly allied cities now being enemies, Dos Pilas still used many symbols and emblems of Tikal throughout their conflict. Many scholars believe that the rulers of Dos Pilas had ambitions of taking the throne of Tikal.

In 672, Tikal attacked Dos Pilas, taking over the city and forcing many of its rulers into exile. Calakmul intervened and began to consolidate its alliance system with the hope that it could fully encircle Tikal and its territory.

In 677, Calakmul attacked Dos Pilas, taking over the city and reinstating the former king on the throne. Two years later, an allied force of Dos Pilas and Calakmul defeated Tikal in a major battle, though this victory did not seem to have a large impact on the Tikal-Calakmul conflict.

Decline

The city constructed five different stelae in the early 740s. By this time, the political power of Calakmul was a fraction of what it once was. Throughout the lowlands, many of Calakmul's most loyal allies were defeated by Tikal. Calakmul's rulers' political power was wholly dependent on this strong alliance system, and as it began to crumble, the city began to decline too.

One of the stela found in Calakmul; this one is dated to the 730s. (Credit: Thelmadatter)

Throughout the Terminal Classic period, Calakmul began to focus on trade from its surrounding area in the central lowlands to the northern Yucatan. This may indicate that the Calakmul government foresaw the region's decline and hoped to stay afloat by establishing relationships with growing cities in the north like Chichen Itza.

The last structures of any kind that were built in Classic Calakmul were three stelae constructed in 810, which is around the time historians believe the city's government completely collapsed. During this period, cities that Calakmul once ruled increasingly began to erect their own cultural monuments and break away from the distinctive cultural practices of their former overlords.

There is evidence that a small population, maybe even part of the ruling class, stayed in the city after it was heavily depopulated throughout the 9th century. Some monuments were built, but they were very crudely constructed compared to the Classic period monuments. This may have been an attempt to reinvigorate the city and bring it back to what it once was.

After centuries of political domination in the central and southern lowlands, by the Terminal Classic period, the great cities of Calakmul and Tikal were abandoned ruins hidden amongst the vast Central American rainforest.

Out of all of the great cities of the Classic period, it has puzzled historians why the two greatest cities collapsed so quickly and were never populated again. A large part was certainly the centuries of warfare, as constant fighting surely drained the cities economically.

Historians are still unsure of what exactly led to the abrupt deterioration of Calakmul and the other Classic cities, but a growing body of evidence points to a few likely causes. The following chapter will discuss the numerous theories and evidence that point to why the two giants of the lowlands collapsed.

Chapter 8: The Collapse of the Classic Era

Between the 8th and 9th centuries, the Maya cities of the southern lowlands were rapidly depopulated. This period has been called the "Classic Maya Collapse," as the Classic Maya period was replaced by the Postclassic Maya period. The 9th century is often classified as the Terminal Classic period.

While many theories have been made about the collapse, experts are unsure of what exactly led to the disintegration of urban Maya society in the lowlands. There is evidence that the region's great cities, including Tikal, Calakmul, and Palenque, deteriorated throughout the 8th and 9th centuries and then were soon completely abandoned.

During this period of decline, there were no writings made on monuments and no large construction projects that were conducted within the cities. However, this collapse did not bring an end to the Maya civilization.

In fact, as the great cities of the southern lowlands began to fail, the cities of the northern Yucatan filled the power vacuum and began to prosper as the new dominating cities of the Maya world. Many of these new cities in the north carried over many cultural traditions and characteristics of the Classic Maya, though many artistic styles were left in the past.

The city of Chichen Itza became the dominant power of the peninsula during the collapse, and many other cities both in both the northern Yucatan and the highlands to the south prospered up until the Spanish conquests. While this period is often referred to as the "Maya Collapse," many Mesoamerican experts reject this terminology. They believe instead that the power that culminated in the cities of the southern lowlands shifted and dispersed out throughout the region.

Theories of the Collapse

Mesoamerican scholars have suggested almost one hundred different theories, and they have not been able to reach a consensus on a unified explanation. However, a number of themes seem to be accepted by the academic community as contributing factors to the collapse.

A collapse of the Maya's urban centers due to environmental factors tends to be one of the leading theories. Many scholars believe that a severe drought or series of droughts in the region caused the sudden decline. Another theory that scholars have explored is an invasion by the Toltecs of Central Mexico or another outsider cultural group. However, most scholars do not believe that there is enough evidence that a military invasion collapsed Maya society by itself.

Mesoamerican scholars have continually proposed a theory that the overland trade routes that dominated the lowlands, which made cities like Tikal and Calakmul economic hubs of trade, were replaced by overseas trade routes that traveled around the peninsula. The abandonment of the lowland trade routes may have been caused by the constant warfare of the region, as many merchants surely would have chosen to travel by sea than trek through the war-torn lowlands. This would have shifted the power dynamic of the Yucatan Maya away from the southern and central lowlands to the coastal region. The dissolution of trade routes that connected the Maya people for centuries would have surely led to the deterioration of the cities in the region.

A large, widespread drought that enveloped the region is the most commonly accepted theory among Mesoamerican scholars. Modern research has shown that the region saw a 40% decrease in annual rainfall during the Terminal period. A drought would have inhibited the population from cultivating agriculture, which the cities had become wholly reliant on, and damaged many of the fertile soils throughout the lowlands. While the central cities would have begun to collapse quickly during a prolonged drought, the cities near the coast like Chichen Itza would have been much less affected by the drought, as they have relatively more freshwater sources.

While many people think of the Maya heartland as a tropical rainforest with an abundance of annual abundance, the region was especially prone to prolonged drought and had very few freshwater sources. Many environmentalists today are amazed that the Maya people thrived in such an inhospitable region of the world.

The Maya combatted their lack of permanent freshwater sources by many ingenious methods of collecting rainwater. However, a severe prolonged drought may have made these water storage practices untenable for the large populations of the cities. Also, there is clear evidence that these water supplies were heavily polluted by the time of the collapse.

The Maya were some of the most advanced agriculturalists in the world, as they used a variety of techniques and innovations to cultivate the land to feed the large populations of the urban cities. However, the use of slash-and-burn agricultural practices would have led to immense deforestation throughout the Maya heartland. This immense, widespread environmental degradation would have taken the forests decades to recover.

There is also some evidence of revolution or rebellion by the populations of the cities against their rulers. Many sacred monuments and structures were defaced and damaged around the time of the collapse, which may point to the population symbolically destroying the sacred structures of the ruling class before abandoning the cities.

The cities that came to power after the Classic collapse show a much less "divine worship" of their rulers, and it seems that the Postclassic populations sought more pragmatic, secular governments than those of the Classic. As drought, deforestation, and warfare enveloped the region, it would make sense that the Classic populations would quickly turn on their rulers, who preached that they were divinely put on the throne by the gods to protect their people.

While Mesoamerican scholars have been searching for a primary theory on the Classic Maya collapse, the collapse of the classic cities of the lowlands was most likely caused by a combination of environmental, economic, and political factors that may never be fully understood.

Despite the popular belief that the collapse brought an end to the Maya civilization, many regions of the Maya heartland prospered after the 10th century, especially on the peninsula's northern coast.

What has puzzled many scholars is why the central and southern lowlands weren't repopulated after the collapse. The Classic Maya urban centers were characterized by a constant cycle of development, collapse, and disbursement. After many examples of "collapses," most notably during the Preclassic period, the Maya people disbursed elsewhere in the region, and soon new urban centers emerged.

However, the southern and central lowlands would never be densely populated again after the collapse, making historians wonder where these people went. The populations that left these cities most likely moved north through the Yucatan towards the Atlantic coast, while others traveled east and west, joining other Mesoamerican societies.

Water storage methods, along with many other administrative innovations, had become extremely complex by the Classic period. The repopulation of the region would have entailed a complete reconstruction of these water storage systems, a massive labor-intensive project that may not have seemed worthwhile. There may have also been a religious or spiritual element, as many may have chosen not to return because they believed the gods condemned the cities.

As the great cities like Tikal collapsed in the south, the northern cities like Chichen Itza filled the power vacuum and carried forward the torch of the Classic Maya. However, the Classic Maya collapse undoubtedly brought an end to the centuries-long progression from primitive agrarian villages to the great temples of Tikal and Cakamral. The collapse of the Classic Maya cities of the lowlands did not mean the collapse of the Maya civilization, but it would never be the same.

The artistic and cultural achievements of the Classic Maya were swallowed up by the jungle and left behind as the population dispersed elsewhere. During the Postclassic period, the Maya people would undergo a series of enormous transformations as they tried to fill the void that the collapse created.

Chapter 9: Chichen Itza: The Wonder City

The city of Chichen Itza was located in the modern-day Tinúm Municipality of the Yucatán State of Mexico, located in the northern Yucatan Peninsula. Chichen Itza was considered one of the largest pre-Colombian Maya cities and came to be one of the most prosperous cities of the Yucatan during the Terminal Classic period.

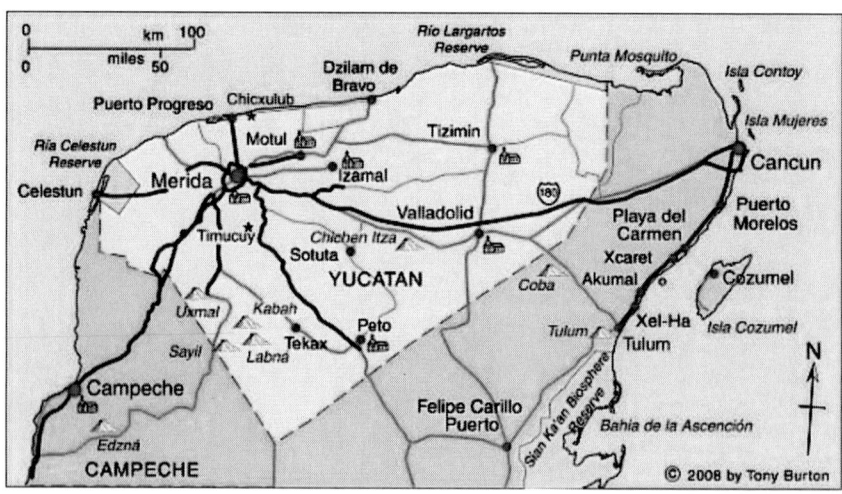

A map of the upper Yucatan Peninsula. (Credit: Geo-Mexico)

Some experts believe that the city had an especially diverse population, which would reflect the city's diversity of artistic and architectural styles. This was mostly caused by an influx of Maya migrants from cities like Tikal that traveled north towards the coast after the collapse of the Classic period.

Four different sinkholes, or "cenotes," served as the main freshwater sources for the city's population. There has also been evidence that the cenotes were used for human sacrifice to the rain god Chaac, as found in the most famous of the cenotes, the Cenote Sagrado. Many sacred objects that are commonplace in Maya burials, such as jade, were found in these sinkholes, along with human remains. Most of the human remains found were of children.

The Cenote Sagrado ("Sacred Cenote"). It has been suggested that many of the human sacrifices were killed prior to being thrown in the cenote. Since only some cenotes held human remains, it is possible the Maya believed certain cenotes led to the underworld. (Credit: Salhedine)

The name Chichen Itza translates to "at the mouth of the well of the Itza," which probably refers to the large cenotes and the heavy influence of Itza culture in the city. While Itza-Puuc styles characterize the architecture of the northern part of the city, the southern part of the city is heavily influenced by Toltec styles. Some scholars have hypothesized that this was caused by a large migration or possible invasion by the Toltecs. However, most believe that it simply reflects interaction with the great Toltec city of Tula.

From the early 10th to the mid-11th century, Chichen Itza rose to prominence as the most prosperous city of the Yucatan Peninsula, boasting a population of 35,000. During its height of power, the city took advantage of its prime location on the coast of the northern Yucatan Peninsula and became an important economic power of the Maya lowland trade routes.

The city created Isla Cerritos as one of the most important Central American ports. As the southern and central lowlands erupted into constant warfare throughout the Classic period, many trade routes were disrupted. Overseas trade routes around the peninsula instead of across it became more common, giving cities near the coast like Chichen Itza a great economic advantage. With its close proximity to the sea, merchants of Chichen Itza were able to sail throughout the Gulf of Mexico, obtaining items that were rare to the Yucatan region, such as gold and obsidian from Central Mexico.

The Layout of the City

The most prominent structures of the city center covered an area of around two square miles, making it one of the largest urban centers in the northern Yucatan. The engineers of the city leveled out the ground in the center of the city in order to construct many of the city's greatest structures.

The city had many causeways, or streets, which connected the various sections of the city to the central plaza. The city was full of stone buildings that formed different functions, ranging from residential homes to administrative buildings used by the government. The structures of the southern part of the city, called "Old Chichen," had many characteristics of the Puuc style of architecture that originated in the central Yucatan lowlands.

El Castillo, a 98-foot pyramid located in the center of the city, is the most prominent architectural project of Chichen Itza. Not only was the construction of the structure an impressive architectural feat, but it also highlights the sophistication of their knowledge of astronomy and timekeeping.

A picture of El Castillo, also known as the Pyramid of Kukulkan. (Credit: Daniel Schwen)

The pyramid was constructed with four sides that each had 91 stairs and faced every cardinal direction. The four sides and their staircases add up to 365, the total number of days in the year. During the equinoxes of autumn and spring, a large shadow taking a snake's shape is cast down the stairs. A large inscription of a snake is located at the top of the pyramid, representing one of the Maya's gods. El Castillo was built on top of another older temple dedicated to the jaguar god of the underworld. By the Classic period, this was a common practice in Maya cities.

The detail and thought put into the construction of El Castillo show the great breadth of knowledge and beliefs that permeated Maya society and how it intertwined with their great architectural feats.

Excavations have shown that a great marketplace existed below the pyramids, suggesting that the large plaza was used for large crowds to watch rituals take place at the top of the pyramid and congregate with fellow citizens and shop.

The Caracol, a large structure used as an observatory for the city's astronomers, was constructed sometime before the 9th century. Many scholars believe that this building was used to view Venus and may have been dedicated to Kukulkan, the Maya wind god.

The Temple of the Warriors is a complex that was built sometime between the 9th and 11th centuries. The temple walls were decorated with large depictions of Maya warriors and battle and has many inscriptions of feathered serpents. The temple closely resembles a similar found in the Toltec capital city of Tula, which has led many historians to suggest that there was considerable cultural diffusion between the two cities.

The Temple of the Warriors. The murals inside the complex depict battles and warriors. (Credit: Keith Pomakis)

Chichen Itza is also home to the largest ball court of Mesoamerica, at 545 feet long and 223 feet wide. There are many inscriptions on the walls of the court showing victorious players displaying the decapitated heads of their opponents.

There are numerous theories on how the ballgame was played. Most believe that the game's goal was to keep the ball from hitting the ground by hitting it against the walls, most likely with the players' hips. The ball used was made of rubber and could weigh up to nine pounds. While the game was most likely played often recreationally by the city's population, the inscriptions at the ball court of Chichen Itza indicate that there may have been a ritualistic element to the game.

The ball court at Chichen Itza. (Credit: Bjørn Christian Tørrissen)

Overlooking the ball court, the Temple of the Jaguar is a large temple complex with many inscriptions of the Maya feathered serpent deities and a large depiction of a battle. In the lower temple of the complex, there is a throne decorated with an inscription of a jaguar figure, similar to the throne in El Castillo.

Adjacent to the Great Ball Court was the Temple of the Bearded Man, a small temple that has an inscription of a large, bearded man. Right across from the Temple of the Bearded Man is a larger structure, but it was destroyed beyond recognition.

Maya Blue and Sacrifice

During the heyday of the city, these buildings would have been painted in an array of festive colors. The Chichen Itza metropolis would have looked much different from the drab stone ruins found at the modern site.

One of the most popular colors used throughout Maya cities like Chichen Itza was "Maya Blue." The pigment was used throughout cities on sculptures, pottery, and murals. The turquoise color comes from the combination of indigo plant material and palygorskite ore. These ingredients were combined in small kilns at high temperatures of up to 200 degrees Celsius. The pigment is extremely resilient and long-lasting, as many murals and objects still have visible traces of the color despite centuries of erosion.

An example of Maya artwork that uses Maya Blue. (Credit: Constantino Reyes)

Maya artists began using the color to paint murals during the latter part of the Preclassic era, and the use of the pigment soon began to spread to monuments, stelae, and pottery throughout the cities. It was the main color of Chaak, the rain deity, who also happened to be the central figure in Maya human sacrifices.

When the city priests anticipated a drought, they would often choose a victim for either nonlethal bloodletting or, in more dire cases of drought, human sacrifice. To appease Chaak, a victim would be fully painted with the pigment and sacrificed in the city's central plaza.

The extent of human sacrifice in the Maya is unknown to scholars, as inscriptions and depictions of the sacrifices left by the Maya have kept the topic a mystery in terms of its methods and frequency. Prisoners of war were certainly used most frequently for sacrifices. The victims could have been either beheaded or disemboweled, most likely in a ritualistic ceremony conducted by the city priests. More extreme examples, like being thrown into the Chichen Itza cenotes, were most likely very rare occurrences.

The capturing of kings and other royalty of a rival city often led to public executions and sacrifices. These killings celebrated the political victory of defeating a rival leader and spiritually gave the gods royal blood.

Most sacrifices were likely not lethal, as ceremonial objects and artifacts were symbolically given to the gods as material sacrifices. The practice of "bloodletting" was also frequently practiced when citizens of the city made small, non-lethal cuts on their bodies as a blood sacrifice.

<u>Early History</u>

The city was first populated and constructed between the 6th and 8th centuries and was further developed throughout the 10th and 11th centuries as it grew into a prosperous trading hub for the Yucatan.

Despite its location near the Gulf Coast, the northern Yucatan is considered one of the driest and arid regions of the Maya heartland. Chichen Itza probably became an ideal location for settlers due to the many water supplies located in its natural cave systems and sinkholes.

Rise to power

The city had already risen to prominence by the beginning of the 7th century, as it became a vital regional trade city in the northern lowlands. With the decline of many of the large cities in the south (like Tikal), Chichen Itza became the dominant political, cultural, and economic power of the Maya lowlands during the late 9th century.

Leading up to Chichen Itza's rise to regional dominance, the two neighboring cities of Yaxuna and Coba, who were close allies, both began to decline. Some experts believe that Chichen Itza may have played a direct role in these cities' decline, either by direct intervention or simply out-competing them economically.

After enjoying a period of regional prosperity, the city began to decline around the year 900. During this time, an influx of migrants of the Itza culture from the south arrived in the city and began to revitalize the city's northern half. Throughout the 10th century, the neighboring city of Uxmal, a close ally of Chichen Itza, rapidly declined and paved the way for Chichen Itza to ascend to power once again.

Decline

Evidence shows that by the beginning of the 12th century, the city had declined as a weaker city in the region, marking the rise of the neighboring city of Mayapan. During this period, Chichen Itza allied with both Mayapan and Uxmal, called the League of Mayapan, which will be covered in Part 4.

When the Spanish conquistadors arrived in Chichen Itza, they noted a large population was still living in the city. However, some experts believe that this population may have been living in the outskirts of the city's ruins. The Spanish also noted that the Cenote Sagrado continued to serve as a sacred place for the Maya people.

Chichen Itza today is one of the most visited sites of Mesoamerica due to its many great structures and monuments like El Castillo. While it only maintained its regional dominance of the northern Yucatan for a short time after the Classic Maya collapse, the city proved itself worthy of carrying the torch of the Classic cities to the south.

The breathtaking achievements of the city's population, its blend of Itza and Toltec influences, and its economic prosperity near overseas trade routes showed that despite the collapse of the great Classic cities, the Maya civilization was more alive than ever. The decline of Chichen Itza marked the beginning of a new era in northern Yucatan when the city of Mayapan became the most powerful city in the region.

PART THREE: THE POSTCLASSIC MAYA ERA (900-1511 AD)

Chapter 10: The K'iche' Kingdom of Q'umarkaj

Q'umarkaj

The Kingdom of Q'umarkaj (also called Utatlán in the Maya language) was located in Guatemala's highlands. The city was created by King Q'uq'umatz, which translates to "Feathered Serpent" in the K'iche' language at the beginning of the 15th century.

Q'umarkaj was situated on a large plateau in the Guatemalan highlands, 1.6 miles west of the modern city of Santa Cruz del Quiche. The archaeological site covers an area of 1,300,000 square feet, making it one of the largest sites of the Maya highlands. At its height, the city of Q'umarkaj and its immediate surrounding area had a population of 15,000 people.

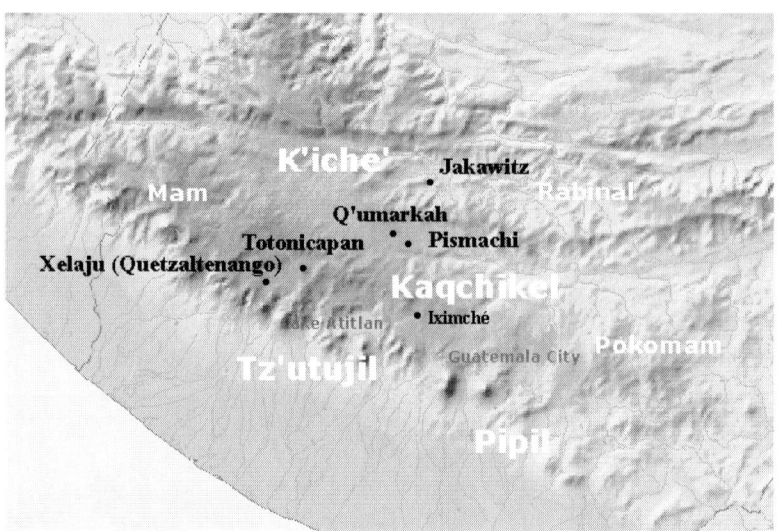

This map shows the important centers of K'iche', which is located in southern Guatemala. (Credit: Maunius)

There was a deeply rooted socioeconomic order in the city, as the K'iche' comprised three different lineages: The Nima were elite ruling class, the Tamub were merchants, and the Ilok'ab were the primary warriors of the K'iche'.

<u>Founding of the City</u>

The exact origin of the K'iche speaking peoples is still up for debate among scholars. Still, most agree that they most likely originated from the Tabasco region of the Gulf Coast of Mexico. These peoples traveled along the Gulf Coast and through the southern lowlands to reach the city, though some scholars believe they may have traveled along the Pacific coast to reach the Guatemalan highlands. Most of these people probably made the journey around Chichen Itza's decline in the northern Yucatan, sometime in the 12th century.

The Layout of the City

The city contained eleven plazas surrounded by an array of temples and complexes, all elevated on a series of terraces. These structures all tend to be around the same size, though the structures surrounding the central plaza are the city's largest structures.

A large series of ditches separated the elite administrative area of the city from the majority of the residential living areas, reflecting the deep socioeconomic divisions in the city. Many of these houses seem to have cultural markers that differ greatly from the elite structures of the city. This has caused many scholars to hypothesize that the city's citizenry was possibly conquered by a population that made themselves the elite ruling class after the conquest and allowed their citizens to retain their cultural identity.

Early History

The K'iche' were a Maya people that had settled in the highlands sometime around 600 BC. There is archaeological evidence that the region was populated to some degree as far back as the Preclassic period, but most of the city's artifacts are dated to the Postclassic. During the Late Postclassic, the area of the city probably had around 15,000 people living in it.

The capitals of the K'iche' kingdom were originally at Jakawitz and then Pismachi, but at the beginning of the 15th-century, King Q'uq'umatz chose the area for its great natural defensive position on the tall plateau. King Q'uq'umatz would maintain a spiritual legacy among the K'iche' people after his death, as he was described as a mythical figure who could transform himself into various animals.

Political Order

The socioeconomic factions within K'iche' society run deep, as the nobles, or "ajaw," claimed to be descendants of foreign invaders from the Gulf Coast that conquered the region during the beginning of the 13th century. The invaders took over the region's political power and abandoned many of their Gulf cultural traditions, fully integrating into the K'iche' culture of their conquered subjects.

The vassals of the K'iche', or "al k'ajol," served as the lower classes of highland society. They served as workers, farmers, and soldiers and usually did not have any opportunities for upward mobility in the political system. The vassals, however, could earn high titles in the military for showing bravery and skill on the battlefield. Merchants were slightly higher on the socioeconomic ladder than the vassals but were forced to pay tributes to the noble class.

The kingdom was ruled by a government comprised of four power powerful figures: the king, king-elect, and two captains. Each of these rulers belonged to the most celebrated lineages of the city.

Expansion

Throughout the 15th century, the K'iche' gradually began expanding their territory throughout the region and created a powerful alliance with the Kaqchikel, a powerful Maya people of the midwestern highlands.

During this period, Q'uq'umatz offered the ruler of the K'oja, a nearby Maya culture of the Cuchumatan mountains, his daughter for marriage. However, instead, the K'oja killed Q'uq'umatz's daughter when she arrived in their territory. This sparked a bloody war between the two cities.

King Q'uq'umatz ultimately died in battle while fighting against the K'oja and was succeeded by his son, K'iq'ab, who vowed to defeat the K'oja. He entered the city of K'oja with a large military force, killed the king, and sacked the city. He also recovered his father's remains and brought a large number of prisoners, as well as many valuable jade artifacts. The K'iche' military also brought many areas near K'oja under their control after the victory.

K'iq'ab continued to bring great prosperity to the kingdom as he went on greatly military conquests that expanded K'iche' territory to the Okos River in the west and the Motagua River to the east.

Decline

As K'iq'ab's territory expanded, civil war broke out at Q'umarkaj as the vassals attempted to overthrow the royal class. Two of K'iq'ab's sons joined in with the vassals, killing many high-ranking nobles of the city. High-ranking members of the allied Kaqchikel warriors were forced to flee back to their territory.

K'iq'ab was nearly killed during the uprising but fled to the city's periphery with some troops that remained loyal to him. The king agreed to make some concessions to the rebels, which created a new noble class of lords. K'iq'ab died soon after in 1475. Despite the great territorial expansion that characterized his reign, the city was much weaker than it was when he ascended the throne, largely due to the internal unrest of the city's political structure and the dissolution of its alliance with Kaqchikel.

Following the death of K'iq'ab, the city became entangled in bloody warfare with its neighbors, including the Tz'tutjil people and its former ally, the Kaqchikel. The K'iche' attempted to conquer the capital city of the Kaqhickel but were defeated. This sparked a sharp decline in the K'iche' military and political power in the region.

By the time Spanish conquistadors arrived in the Guatemalan highlands in 1524, the city of Q'umarkaj was a shadow of what it was during the 15th century. Q'umarka completely drained itself of its former glory due to its dysfunctional internal political system and its hunger for territorial expansion.

Chapter 11: The League of Mayapan

The Mayapan league was formed in 987 AD by Maya ruler Ah Mekat Tutul Xiu. The league was a political alliance between the northern Yucatan cities of Chichen Itza, Mayapan, and Uxmal. The league was centered around the city of Chichen Itza, which was the most powerful city in the region during the Early Postclassic. The league was also comprised of many smaller cities and villages throughout the region, but it is unclear how much power these smaller polities had when it came to governance.

This league was most likely created due to the crumbling of the great Classic cities to the south, as the Maya of the northern Yucatan feared that the increasing warfare could spread to the north or that an influx of desperate migrants would take over the region. The league's creation was also undoubtedly caused by the heavy droughts and disruption of trade routes that characterized the time. The northern Yucatec Maya may have tried to carry forward and implement the most important takeaway of the Classic Maya collapse: that lack of peace, stability, and cooperation caused the decline of the greatest cities of the lowlands. The alliance was created to maintain some semblance of a centralized government in the region, promoting peace and trade among the northern Yucatec Maya.

However, throughout the Postclassic period, the league quickly began to crumble due to internal struggles between the three cities. Mayapan gradually replaced Chichen Itza as the most powerful city of the northern Yucatan.

Mayapan

Mayapan was located 100 kilometers west of Chichen Itza and became the most powerful city of the northern Yucatan from the early 13th to the mid-15th century. Over 4,000 structures have been found throughout its archaeological site, and experts believe up to 17,000 people could have lived in the city during its height.

Mayapan, which translates to "banner of the Maya," served as the last great capital of the Maya in the northern Yucatan and is considered one of the most densely populated cities to ever exist. The city was formed during the 11th century by the Cocom, an elite family from Chichen Itza that fled due to political rivalry.

The Temple of Kukulkan. It is similar to the one at Chichen Itza, although archaeologists consider the latter to be far superior in terms of craftsmanship. (Credit: Pavel Vorobiev)

The city was abandoned abruptly during the mid-15th century, and there is evidence that part of the city may have been burned to the ground. Archaeological evidence points to increased warfare in the northern Yucatan throughout the 14th and 15th centuries, and by Mayapan's decline, large defensive fortifications had been constructed around the city.

Uxmal

Uxmal was a powerful city in the northern Yucatan region from around 850 to 900 AD during the Terminal Classic period. Beginning around the year 1000, the city's population began to leave the city, possibly migrating to the nearby cities of Chichen Itza and Mayapan. By 1200 the city was nearly abandoned.

The city was founded by the Tutal Xiues, a Maya people that traveled eastward from the Gulf Coast to the northern Yucatan sometime during the Late Classic. The city most likely joined the League of Mayapan during its decline, making it the weakest city in the alliance.

Toltec Influence and Possible Invasion

The architectural layout of Chichen Itza has long been a hot topic for debate among Maya scholars, with some believing that the presence of Toltec influences in the city may point to a Toltec invasion of the northern Yucatan urban centers. Both the cities of Mayapan and Uxmal also had many Toltec architectural/cultural characteristics, which many point to the League of Mayapan forming partly due to a shared Toltec cultural heritage.

Many scholars who worked in the Carnegie Institution of Washington research programs of the mid-20th century concluded that before the possible Postclassic invasion, Chichen Itza was populated by a different Maya cultural group, meaning that the Itzas would eventually take over the city during the Postclassic were the Toltecs from Tulla.

However, recent scholarship has largely disproved this theory. Most academic scholars now maintain that the Itza of Chichen Itza simply had great trading and diplomatic relations with the Toltec of Tulla, which shaped their cultural and architectural styles.

Dissolution of the League

By 1175 the league began to unravel. While archaeology has not yet proven the following narrative of the league's dissolution, it is cited in multiple Maya sources and is accepted by many Mesoamerican scholars.

Ceel Cauich Ah was thrown into the sacred cenote of Chichen Itza and somehow managed to survive. Due to the sacred nature of the cenote to the Maya people, Ceel Cauich Ah proclaimed himself the divine ruler of the region. Most of Chichen Itza's population did not accept him as ruler, while much of Mayapan's population did.

Upon the league's dissolution, Chichen Itza was replaced by Mayapan as the greatest city of the northern peninsula. The city of Uxmal declared war on the Cocom people of Mayapan in 1441, officially bringing an end to the league.

Chapter 12: Peten Itza: The Last Maya Kingdom

The last great Maya kingdom was the kingdom of Peten Itza, revolving around the city of Nojpetén. Twenty-one sacred temples have been throughout the city's archaeological site. The city was considered one of the central centers of the Itza during the Postclassic period.

The city was isolated on an island in Lake Petén, and it appears that no bridges or other structures connected the city to the rest of the lowlands. The city remained relatively politically and diplomatically isolated, as it only had relationships with the Itza cities of Chakok'at, Ch'ich, and Chakan. By the time of the Spanish conquests, an estimated 60,000 people lived in the city.

The location of Peten Itza (Credit: Mabarlabin)

Lake Peten is the largest body of water in the Maya heartland and was the home for the Itza Maya people for centuries. The Peten lakes region comprised a group of eight large lakes linked together that stretched 80 kilometers from east to west. The freshwater sources of the river are a small number of seasonal streams that flow throughout the area. By far, the largest lake in the region is Lake Peten Itza, which covers an area of around 100 kilometers.

<u>The Itza People</u>

The Itza were not a single unified cultural people but were instead made up of many different powerful family clans that ruled the area. The Itza also had great influence in the cities of Chichen Itza and Mayapan in the northern Yucatan during the Postclassic. A great proportion of the Itza population from these northern regions most likely migrated southwards to the lake during the decline of Chichen Itza and Mayapan leading up to the arrival of the Spanish.

Both the northern and southern Itza were known as some of Mesoamerica's greatest merchants, overseeing long-distance trade routes from Central Mexico to southern regions of Central America.

The Itza people most likely originated in the Peten Basin of the southern lowlands, with a large proportion of their population migrating up to the northern Yucatan during the collapse of the lowlands, and then a large wave of Itza migrants moving back down to Peten following the collapse of the League of Mayapan.

The academic community has yet to reach a consensus on the origins of the Itza as a unified kingdom and when they began to gain political influence in the Peten lakes. Multiple inscriptions found in Maya cities in modern-day Belize, as well as northern cities like Chichen Itza, seem to mention interactions with an Itza leader during the Late Classic period.

The Peten Itza Government

By the time of the arrival of the Spanish during the 16th century, the Peten region had become a well-organized, hierarchical political region that was ruled by a series of elite Itza families, greatly resembling the governmental structures of the northern Itza cities like Chichen Itza.

Many historians believe that the widespread influence of the Itzas in both the northern and southern lowlands hints at a great military force that integrated their conquered people into Itza society. After conquering a population, they most likely encouraged them to marry into elite families, which would allow some of the conquered peoples to become high-ranking royalty in Itza society. This not only gave the Itza conqueror large, already well-established cities and populations to expand on but also diminished the likelihood of rebellion or political unrest within their governmental structures. By making their conquered peoples a powerful part of the Itza government, the Itza were able to spread their influence throughout the Maya heartland without alienating or decimating populations of fellow Mayas.

The ruler of the Peten Itza people throughout the 16th and 17th centuries was always given the title of "Ajaw Kan Ek" in Spanish records. He lived in the capital island city of Nojpetén and held the highest governmental position of the entire Peten region.

The governments of the Itza provinces were generally comprised of eight people. These eight officials were divided into junior-senior pairs based on the cardinal directions. For example, the governing council of one of the western provinces would consist of a senior official who oversaw the affairs of the province, while a junior official oversaw the largest town in that province.

The larger Itza confederacy, which acted as a unified kingdom of the Peten region, was comprised of a governing council made up of the four senior provincial officials, along with thirteen "ach kats" that ruled the small settlements throughout the periphery of the confederacy.

The full territory controlled by the Itzas during their height of power is not yet fully known, though it is clear that they were some of the region's greatest agriculturalists, with fields stretching throughout the central-southern lowlands.

Spanish Contact

After conquering the Aztec Empire of Central Mexico, Spanish conquistador Hernan Cortes traveled through the Peten Itza region. In March 1525, the expeditionary force arrived on the shore of Lake Peten Itza, where ruler Aj Kan Ek received him'. After witnessing Catholic mass, Aj Kan Ek' immediately converted to Christianity and invited the men into the city of Nojpeten.

After the encounter, no other Spanish forces attempted to enter the Peten Basin for nearly a century, mostly due to its impenetrable jungle cover. In 1618 two Spanish missionaries departed the settlement of Merida to convert the Itza of the Peten. The ruler of Peten Itza welcomed the missionaries but refused to abandon the native Maya religion. After one of the missionaries attempted to destroy a statue of a deity, the native population began to grow agitated at the visitors. Only after one of the missionaries conducted a peaceful sermon did the natives calm down. The Spaniards left soon after and established a friendly relationship with the ruler of the Peten Itza.

The next year the missionaries returned to Lake Peten and were again well-received by the ruler. However, the city's priests increasingly saw the Spanish as a threat to their religion and persuaded the ruler to banish them from the kingdom. A Maya military force suddenly surrounded the living quarters of the missionaries, and the Spaniards were forced to leave downriver on a canoe.

After the failed attempts at evangelization, Spanish Captain Francisco de Mirones set out to conquer Peten Itza in 1622. A missionary named Diego Delgado also traveled with the force but became increasingly disillusioned by the treatment of the indigenous peoples by the conquistadors. Delgado split off from Mirones with his own expeditionary force, largely made up of evangelized Mayas from the eastern lowlands. Upon entering the city of Nojpeten, which had not encountered Christian missionaries since 1618, they were immediately taken as prisoners and then sacrificed to the gods. Upon the arrival of Mirones, he and his men were found unarmed in a nearby church by the Peten Itza warriors and were slaughtered. These two failed missions in Peten Itza halted all Spanish attempts to conquer or evangelize the region until 1695.

In 1695 Martín de Ursúa y Arizmendi, the governor of the Yucatan province, began to construct a road from the western Yucatan to Lake Peten. Missionary Andrés de Avendaño traveled on the road and arrived on the shore of Lake Peten to a welcoming group of Itza. The ruler of the Peten Itza arrived the next day, inviting the missionary group into Nojpeten. While in the city, Avendaño baptized many of the city's children and made several attempts to convert the Peten Itza ruler. The ruler said that the time was not right for their conversion and that Avendaño should return in a few months to successfully evangelize the population. The ruler discovered a plot devised by a faction within the city to kill Avendaño and quickly advised them to leave the city.

In December of that year, the Itza ruler sent messengers to Merida to surrender to the Spanish crown. Conquistador Pedro de Zubiaur traveled to Peten with a small military force but was ambushed by a large Maya force. Many of the Spaniards were killed or taken prisoner, and when a relief force arrived the next day, they were too beaten by the Maya warriors. After this failed conquest, Martín de Ursúa began to plan for a massive attack on the Peten Itza region.

Ursúa led his army to Lake Peten in 1697, and the Peten ruler immediately sent a group of envoys that surrendered to the Spaniards. Ursúa accepted the surrender and invited the ruler to visit his camp on the lakeshore the next day. However, the next day, instead of the scheduled arrival of the ruler, a massive force of Maya warriors began to surround the Spanish camp. Now knowing that the only way to conquer the region was with military force, Ursúa led his men on an assault of Nojpeten. Many of the city's defenders died in the ensuing battle for the island, and the Spanish took very few casualties. Ursúa renamed the city "Our Lady of Remedy and Saint Paul, Lake of the Itza."

PART FOUR: SPANISH CONTACT AND CONQUEST (1511-1697 AD)

Chapter 13: First Encounters and Yucatan Exploration

During the Late Postclassic period, Spanish forces reached the Yucatan Peninsula. They began a strategy of herding the local Maya into small colonial settlements that probably resembled modern concentration or internment camps. Many of the Maya either fled into remote areas of the rainforest or joined in with other cities that the Spanish had not yet conquered.

The diverse, ruptured political order of the Maya Yucatan presented a challenge to the Spanish conquistadors, as there was not a central city, state, or authority that could be overthrown, as seen with the Aztecs of Central Mexico. Instead, the Spanish were forced to conquer the region city by city, village by village. The Spanish tackled this problem by taking advantage of political rivalries between Maya populations, making alliances that pit the cities against each other.

The Maya who chose to resist fought a guerilla war against the Spanish invaders and their allies, largely using hit-and-run ambush tactics. While the Spanish had vastly superior weaponry, including small artillery, steel swords, and cavalry, the Maya warriors proved to be fierce fighters who used the terrain of the region to their advantage. The Spanish cavalry became the largest determining factor in battles throughout the conquests. Spanish cavalry charges were extremely effective against fellow European armies, but against the Maya (who had never seen horses before), these charges often caused an immediate, frenzied retreat.

Even more deadly than the Spanish invaders themselves was the plethora of diseases they brought to the region. Diseases like smallpox, measles, and eventually malaria ravaged the local populations throughout the Americas, and both the Maya highlands and lowlands saw enormous mortality rates from these diseases throughout the 16th century.

Biases

The following chapters will explore the Spanish conquests of the Maya heartland: a time period when the Maya people got their first bitter taste of European colonialism as the Spanish attempted to conquer an indigenous population that fought ferociously for the survival of both its culture and people.

It should be noted that most of what is known about these conquests comes from Spanish sources, which tended to have a Euro-centric bias towards depicting the Maya as savages who needed to be civilized by high European culture. (Just as the Maya made biased historical records that depict the Spanish as murderous brutes.) We will never know the full extent of Spanish atrocities against the Maya people, nor the full accuracy of the Spanish depictions of Maya "savagery," such as human sacrifice.

However biased these sources may be, they are unfortunately the only way to begin to understand the conquests of the Americas. How accurate these details, stories, and depictions are may never be fully known. However, by giving a detailed, objective narrative from both Spanish and Maya sources, a general overview of this period of enormous transformation and change in the Maya civilization can begin to be uncovered.

First Encounters

It is believed that the first time the Spanish encountered the Maya of the Yucatan was in 1502 when an expedition led by famed Spanish explorer Christopher Columbus encountered Maya traders off the coast of the peninsula.

Columbus landed on the island of Guanaja off the coast of Honduras during his fourth expedition to the Americas. He then sent his younger brother, Bartholomew Columbus, to explore the island and its waters. While scouting out the region, Bartholomew encountered a large canoe that was being driven by a Maya crew from the Yucatan Peninsula. Many luxury goods were on board, making it very likely it was a trading canoe that was traveling south to trade with other Mesoamerican societies.

Instead of trying to exchange information with the Maya crew or establish a cordial relationship, the Spanish crew instead looted the canoe and took the captain as a prisoner, with hopes that he could serve as an interpreter for future conquest. This first encounter between the Spaniards and Maya would set the grim tone for decades of conquest and exploitation throughout the Yucatan.

The remaining crew traveled back to the peninsula and began to spread the word of their encounter with the Spanish. The news began to spread through coastal Maya cities of the white invaders, and many began to believe they were sent by the feathered serpent god Kukulkan, a powerful deity of the northern lowlands.

In 1511, the "Santa Maria de la Barca" was shipwrecked off the coast of Jamaica in the Caribbean Sea. Captain Pedro de Valdivia and his crew decided to float westward on one of the ship's small boats. Over the course of two weeks, half of the crew died from dehydration and heat exposure. The survivors landed on the eastern coast of the Yucatan, where a not-so-welcoming reception awaited them.

According to Spanish sources, the local Maya lord, Halach Uinik, took the surviving crew as prisoners. The captain and four other crew members were immediately killed in a ritualistic sacrifice, and the local population ate their bodies.

Aguilar and Guerrero

Two of the survivors, Geronimo de Aguilar and Gonzalo Guerrero, escaped from their Maya captors but were captured by another Maya lord. The two men served as slaves in the Maya town of Chetumal for eight years, eventually becoming fluent in the Maya language. Aguilar was eventually rescued by a Spanish expeditionary force led by Hernan Cortes, whom he served as a translator for during his campaigns in Central Mexico.

Guerrero followed a much different path towards freedom. By the time Aguilar was rescued, Guerrero had been partially assimilated into the local Maya culture. He had become a high-ranking member of the Maya town's military force and had taken on many cultural practices of the local population, including traditional Maya piercings and tattoos. He had married a local Maya woman and may have been the first father of mestizo mixed children in the Americas.

Guerrero's fellow Spaniards made several attempts to retrieve him, but he refused to leave the Maya village. There is evidence that Guerrero may have even led campaigns of the local Maya in their fight against his former comrades.

A statue of Guerrero in Akumal, Mexico. (Credit: Wikimedia Commons)

Francisco Hernández de Córdoba

The first Spanish expeditionary force to land on the peninsula was under the command of Francisco Hernández de Córdoba. The fleet departed from Cuba in 1517 and arrived near the northern coast of the peninsula. Córdoba chose not to land due to the dangerous coastal shallows but spotted a small indigenous settlement on the coast. Several Maya canoes rowed out to the ship the next day and had a friendly exchange with the Spanish crew after boarding the vessel.

Deciding that the local population would welcome his forces peacefully, Córdoba decided to land on the shore. The small expeditionary force began to journey to the local city when local Maya warriors attacked them. Some of the crew were wounded by arrows from the ambush, but they were able to successfully push back the Maya attackers. The Maya often used flint arrowheads, meaning they would often shatter inside wounds and cause horrible infections, which would later cause the deaths of two of the wounded men.

After successfully fighting off the attackers, the Spanish forces moved on to the fringes of the nearby city, where they sacked some of the Maya temples and other buildings. The Spaniards found many gold items, which filled the men with great excitement for the riches that could be found in the region. After taking two prisoners to serve as interpreters, Córdoba and his men returned to their ship to continue their expedition.

As the fleet sailed southward down the western coastline of the peninsula, the crew grew dangerously low on their freshwater supplies. The crew arrived at the coastal Maya city of Campeche in February 1517 and immediately sent a party into the city to retrieve water. The city's population allowed them to enter the city and take some water in their casks, but the situation soon soured as the leaders of the city ordered them to return to their ship.

The ship continued sailing southwards for over a week, eventually landing near the Maya city of Champotón. Upon landing on the coast, the crew quickly found a freshwater source but were soon met by a group of warriors from the city. The ship was able to replenish its water supply, but the expeditionary force found itself completely surrounded by a significant Maya force by the next day.

During the hour-long battle that ensued, over half of the Spanish force was killed, and every surviving Spaniard was wounded. At the end of the battle, the surviving men made a frantic scramble to their ships and set sail for the Caribbean.

The story of the expedition was documented by Captain Córdoba, who succumbed to his wounds shortly after the battle at Champotón. More importantly, he also wrote in detail about the gold and other wealthy artifacts found in the Maya region. While the narrative of this expedition did not have a happy ending for the first Spaniards to explore the Maya heartland, it did not deter further expeditions. The prospects of potential untouched wealth in the Maya territory only further heightened the growing fervor of Spanish conquest in the Americas.

Juan de Grijalva

In 1518, Juan de Grijalva was sent by his uncle, Cuban Governor Diego Velázquez, on the second expedition to the Yucatan. Velázquez was highly optimistic about the reports of gold on the coastal areas of the peninsula and gave his nephew four ships for the expedition.

In April 1518, the fleet arrived on the island of Cozumel off the eastern Yucatan coast. Grijalva and his men made several attempts to interact with the island's population, but then they fled from the coast upon the arrival of the ships. After cruising down the peninsula's east coast, Grijalva decided to turn back and sail down the western coast.

The force reached the city of Campeche and attempted to negotiate a trade for drinking water, but the city's population declined. The angered captain then opened fire on the city with a mounted cannon, which caused much of the population to abandon the city and flee into the forest. While the fleet was approaching Champotón, a band of Maya warriors in canoes appeared, but they quickly fled to shore when Grijalva began firing his cannons.

The fleet then sailed to the Tabasco region of the Gulf Coast, where a group of Maya warriors stared at them from the coastline but did not show any signs of attack. Grijalva used his translators to conduct a small trade transaction with the group, who told him about the great wealth of the Aztecs in Central Mexico. The fleet then sailed west to the Central Mexican coastline and saw many signs of the great Aztec Empire.

On their voyage back to the Caribbean to report on the great Aztec Empire, the fleet stopped at Champotón to avenge the Spaniards killed at the city during the previous expedition. The ensuing battle had similar results as the first, and a large number of the expeditionary force was wounded and forced to flee back to their ships.

While these two expeditions only resulted in brief encounters with coastal Maya populations, they sowed the seeds for the ensuing conquests that would ravage Maya society. The immense untouched wealth of Mesoamerica was confirmed by these perilous voyages, and now it was only a matter of time before the great conquistadors of the 15th century arrived to take it.

Chapter 14: Hernan Cortes and Pedro de Alvarado

As rumors spread throughout Spain and the Spanish-controlled Caribbean about the potential riches of Mesoamerica, the greatest of the Spanish explorers emerged as the captain of the most ambitious expedition of the Americas yet. Hernan Cortes was captivated by stories of the great wealth of the Aztec Empire in Central Mexico. He saw the Yucatan Peninsula as not only a place of great potential wealth itself but also a prime landing location and base of operations for the eventual push to the Aztec heartland.

Cortes was put in charge of an 11-ship fleet and 500 men for the expedition. Many crew members like Pedro de Alvarado would become some of the most famous (or infamous) conquistadors of the Spanish conquests.

An engraving of Cortes by the 19th-century artist William Holl. (Credit: United States Library of Congress)

Cortes' Expedition

Just like the expedition before them, the fleet first arrived at the island of Cozumel. However, Cortes knew that his expedition had to bring a much more permanent element to the Spanish influence of the Americas. Sacred Maya temples were defaced upon arriving on the island, and a Christian cross was raised on their roofs. As mentioned in the previous chapter, Cortes also sent a search party to the peninsula that rescued Geronimo de Aguilar, who would serve as his translator.

The fleet then traveled west around the peninsula, eventually reaching the Tabasco region of the Gulf Coast. The Spanish forces landed at the mouth of what Cortes named the Grijalva River, near the Maya town of Potonchan. Maya warriors emerged from the town, and a great battle ensued, ending with a decisive Spanish victory after immense Maya casualties.

The Fall of the Aztecs

After the battle, Cortes was approached by the defeated Maya nobles, who offered him various goods, including gold items and young Maya women. One of these women, named Marina, would play a critical role in conquering Mexico and the Aztecs.

Marina's father was an Aztec chief, and after his death, she was sold into slavery by her mother. She eventually ended up in the Tabasco region after being sold to the Maya of the Gulf Coast. The combination of her great educational background growing up in a noble Aztec family and her fluency in both the Maya and Aztec languages made her a great asset to Cortes.

The young slave proved to be much more than a translator. She proved to be a tremendous asset to the conquest of Mexico, as she taught the Spaniards about the intricacies of Mesoamerican culture and the geography of the region. She would also become a mistress of Cortes during the voyage, and the couple would have a son together.

After the victory in Tabasco, Cortes led his fleet northwest along the coast into the heart of the Aztec Empire. After defeating the Tlaxcalans and Cholula, Cortes formed a powerful alliance with many Central Mexican peoples that were more than willing to help overthrow their Aztec overlords. Cortes eventually captured the capital city of Tenochtitlan in 1521, renaming it Mexico City. The new city would serve as the capital for New Spain and became the center of Spanish colonialism in the Americas.

Interactions with the Maya in Soconusco

After hearing that the Aztec Empire had fallen so quickly to the Spanish, the Kaqchikel and K'iche' Maya of the highlands both sent their diplomats to proclaim their allegiance to the Spanish rule of Mexico. The following year Cortes sent a scouting party to

Soconusco in the southwest of the Chiapas region in the Serra Madre de Chiapas Mountain Range. Despite the allegiance of the K'iche' and Kaqchickel to Spain, the scouts reported that both Maya kingdoms were attacking peoples in Soconusco that were loyal allies to Spain.

With these two Maya kingdoms potentially disrupting Spanish control of the region, Cortes sent Pedro de Alvarado with a massive military force made up of both Spanish troops and Mesoamerican allies to quell the unrest and fully conquer modern-day Guatemala.

Alvarado had completely conquered the Soconusco region by early 1524. While in most Spanish-controlled regions, the indigenous populations were rounded up into the colonial settlements, the Maya of the highlands were largely allowed to stay in their territory due to their cacao orchards, which were considered one of the most valuable crops of New Spain.

Location of Soconusco. (Credit: FAMSI)

Encomienda

The encomienda system was a hallmark of the brutality and exploitation of the conquests. It was the Spanish crown's answer to not being able to establish a centralized colonial government amongst the hostile indigenous populations of the Americas. The encomienda system permitted Spanish colonists to live in any unconquered land they wished. Of course, this land was usually occupied by local populations that were not keen on having new Spanish rulers.

By settling the territory, they effectively owned it in the eyes of the Spanish crown. They had the responsibility of acting as administrators for the land and its local population, which largely meant protecting them from outside invaders, converting them to Christianity, and establishing other institutions, such as an educational system. However, this system almost always turned exploitative. Colonists usually settled on the land with the aid of a military force, conquering the locals and looting much of their wealth. Local Mayas were taken and sold as slaves or worked in fields with little to no pay. The locals were also forced to give up many of their supplies and provisions, causing widespread famine throughout the local villages.

All of this went unpunished by the colonial authorities, as the encomienda system became a blank check signed by the Spanish crown for unchecked exploitation and atrocity throughout the Americas. Under the guise of "civilizing" the native populations, the Spanish authorities allowed the conquistadors and colonists to freely decimate and exploit the Maya people.

Cortes' Conquest of the Lowlands

With the Soconusco region firmly in Spanish control, Cortes set his sight on modern-day Honduras. Cortes had sent one of his most trusted captains, Cristóbal de Olid, to conquer the region, but Olid went rogue and declared himself ruler of the region independent from New Spain.

Cortes departed from the Aztec heartland in October 1524 with a military force largely made up of indigenous Mexican troops. After passing through the Gulf Tabasco region, Cortes led his men into the dense rainforest of the southern Maya lowlands, passing right by the abandoned ruins of Tikal. In March 1525, the force arrived at Lake Peten Itza and was received by the local Mayas. The Maya king who met Cortes was so impressed with the Catholic priests after they held a small ceremony to celebrate mass that he declared that he and his people would immediately convert to Christianity.

After visiting Nojpeten, Cortes embarked on his most arduous part of the expedition yet. His forces crossed into modern-day Belize in the Maya Mountains, and many men and horses died when they found themselves lost in modern-day eastern Guatemala. The men nearly starved to death before they found a young Maya child that led them to a nearby village. Within a few weeks, Cortes finally reached his destination in Honduras with a fraction of the men he departed Central Mexico with. To his surprise, he found that the territory had been reclaimed for New Spain, as his own men killed the rogue captain.

<u>Conquest of the Highlands</u>

In early 1524, Pedro de Alvarado led Spanish forces through the Pacific coastal plain, eventually reaching the K'iche Maya of the Guatemalan highlands. A K'iche military force desperately tried to stop Alvarado from crossing the Samala River but was ultimately unsuccessful. After crossing the river and sending the Maya into retreat, the Spanish sacked the region's villages.

Alvarado clashed with a formidable defensive force at the city of Xetulul on February 8th, and after defeating the Maya, he raided the city and set up his camp in their central plaza. The Spanish force then moved on to the Sierra Madre mountains, where another Maya force ambushed him. After causing the local warriors to flee, he moved on to the city of Xelaju, whose entire population had fled after hearing about the Spanish entrance into the Sierra Madres.

On February 18th, a massive army of 30,000 K'iche' warriors led an attack on Alvarado, but he successfully repulsed the attack, inflicting heavy casualties on the K'iche' army. After their disastrous defeat, the K'iche' lords sued for peace and asked Alvarado to visit Q'umarkaj. At the local city of Tzakaha, Easter Mass was performed, a church was built, and many of the natives were baptized and converted.

Throughout March, Alvarado and his men resided in a small encampment on the outskirts of Q'umarkaj. Alvarado eventually invited two of the city's most powerful leaders to meet with him at the encampment, and as soon as they arrived, he took them as prisoners. Upon hearing the news of their leaders' capture, the K'iche' launched an assault on the camp but were repulsed. After the successful defense of the camp, Alvarado burned the two leaders alive, attacked the city, and razed it to the ground.

After destroying the city, Alvarado reached out to the nearby Kaqchikel people and proposed an alliance to fight the surviving K'iche' warriors that fled the city. After hearing of Q'umarkaj's destruction, numerous other Maya people throughout the highlands surrendered to Alvarado.

In April, Alvarado and his men entered the city of Iximche and established friendly relations with its Kaqchikel rulers. The kings gave the Spanish force many native Maya troops to help defeat the K'iche' and the Tz'utujil. In July, Alvarado decided to make Iximche the capital of colonial Guatemala, renaming it "St. James of the Knights of Guatemala."

Alvarado then sent two envoys to the Tz'utujil to persuade them to surrender, but both the Spaniards were killed. The Spanish immediately met the Tz'utujil for battle at a local lake with a massive force, including many Kaqchikel soldiers. After a devastating cavalry charge, the Tz'utujil retreated in a frenzy to an island in the lake.

The Spanish then attacked the survivors that fled onto the island, though many Tz'utujil were able to escape by swimming to shore.

After the battle, the Spanish and Kaqchikel marched into the Tz'utujils' capital of Tecpan to find it completely abandoned. The Maya rulers of the city soon sent envoys to Alvarado's camp about their desire to surrender.

The scenery one could see from Tecapan. (Credit: Chensiyuan)

Prelude to the Chiapas Conquest

Conquistador Luis Marín was sent into the Chiapas in 1524 to conduct reconnaissance for the upcoming conquest of the region. He departed from Coatzacoalcos on the Gulf Coast with a small expeditionary force, eventually clashing in battle with a force of Chiapanecos warriors on the Grijalva River. After defeating the Maya force, Marín traveled through a settlement populated by Zinacantecos, who would prove to be some of the most loyal Spanish allies in the Chiapas region.

As Marín neared the city of Chamula, he was approached by a group of Tzotzil Mayas, who welcomed him peacefully. However, when he got closer to the city, he began meeting hostile resistance from local warriors and found that the population had fled with their food supplies. Marín was ambushed by the Chamula warriors, who were placed on the top of a cliff, throwing spears down at the Spanish forces. When Marín and his men finally reached Chamula, they found that it was completely abandoned. The Spaniards rode on to Huixtan, an allied city of the Tzotzil, where the population also deserted the city. After defeating the small defensive force there, the Spanish decided to return to Coatzacoalcos.

Kaqchikel Revolt

Despite the strong alliance between the Kaqchikel rulers and Alvarado, the Kaqhickel increasingly grew disillusioned by the exorbitant tributes of gold demanded by the Spanish. After the Kaqchikel refused to pay, the population quickly abandoned the capital city, anticipating a Spanish attack. The Kaqchikel that now lived in the remote forests of the region began to conduct a guerilla war against the conquistadors.

Marín established a new colonial settlement in the region, but it was soon moved eastward to the Almolonga Valley due to constant attacks by Kaqchikel rebels. The Kaqchikel continued their guerilla war against the Spanish until 1530, when two Kaqchikel rulers finally surrendered to Marín.

Zaculeu

The brother of Pedro de Alvarado, Gonzalo de Alvarado y Contreras, conquered the city of Xinabahul in 1525 with a large military force largely made up of native allied troops. He then moved on to the city of Momostenango, which was swiftly taken by the Spanish forces. After taking Momostenango, his forces trekked to Huehuetenango, where a large Mam Maya army met him. The Spanish forces led a cavalry charge on the warriors, who quickly broke into a frenzied retreat and ran for the forest. After reaching the city, the Spaniards founds it completely abandoned.

The ruler of the Mam heard of the Spanish victory and established a strong defense at the city of Zaculeu as the Spaniards approached. He used his large alliance system of the neighboring Maya peoples to defend the city. Still, Alvarado was able to break through many of the defenses during the initial stages of the battle. The Mam warriors withdrew inside the walled defenses of the city as a large Maya reinforcement force attacked the Spaniards from the north. Alvarado's men quickly decimated the reinforcements, and the Spanish launched a siege on Zaculeu that would last for months. By the time the siege was lifted, most of the population of the city was dead, with many of the starving survivors resorting to cannibalism. After the brutal siege, a large garrison was built in Huehuetenango.

Chapter 15: Conquest of the Chiapas

Pedro de Portocarrero was put in charge of a new conquest into the Chiapas region. In early 1528, his forces created a base of operations at San Cristóbal de Los Llanos, which the Tojolabal Maya people controlled. After creating a garrison there, the force gradually pushed on towards the Ocosingo Valley. Portocarrero's expedition into Chiapas was extraordinarily successful, and by the end of the year, the Spanish controlled nearly all of the highlands of Chiapas.

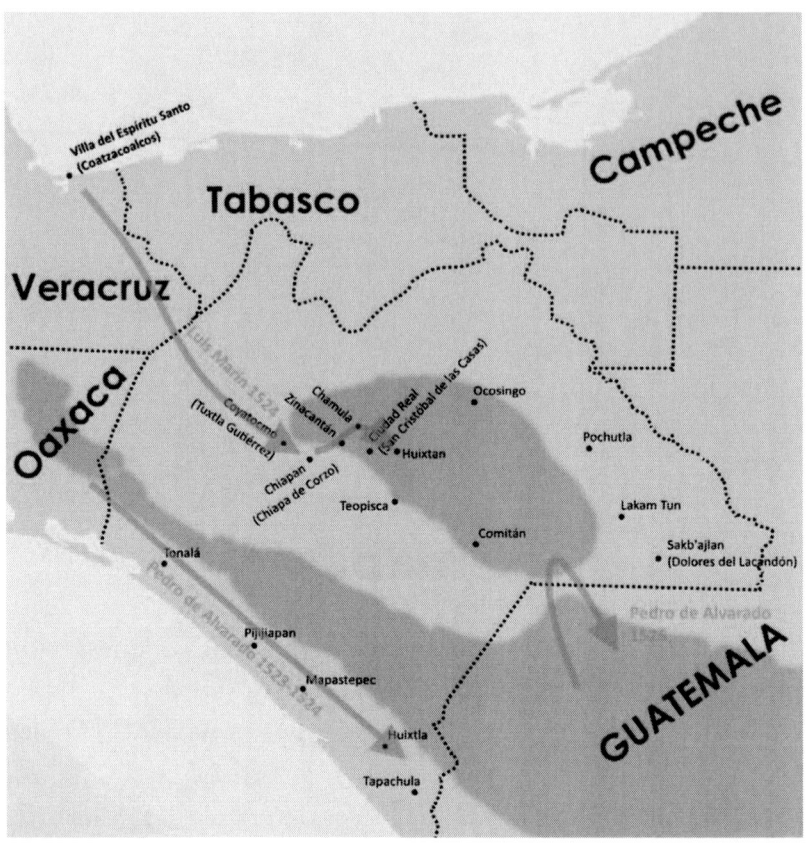

Early entry routes to Chiapas, 1523-1525. (Credit: Simon Burchell)

Diego Mazariegos

That same year, Diego Mazariegos brought a force into the Chiapas region, where much of the population had been killed due to both widespread famine and disease. The local city of Zinacantan, who was complaining about revolts against the new Spanish government, asked for assistance in quelling the rebels, and Mazariegos sent a small force that quickly put down the rebellion.

Mazariegos had been given the orders to turn the highlands of Chiapas into a province for the Spanish crown. After securing Zinacantan, he then led his force to Chiapas, where they created a small garrison called "Villa Real" that would serve as a temporary base of operations for the Chiapas conquest.

Many of the Spaniards who were already in the Chiapas highlands greeted Mazariegos and his men with bitterness, as the region was considered one of the most prized areas of the highlands. Mazariegos ordered Portocarrero and his men to leave the area, and the two men met in the city of Coatzacoalcos to negotiate. It was agreed that the Spanish colonists living in San Cristóbal de Los Llanos would migrate to Villa Real, which was now in the Jovel Valley.

After the negotiations, Portocarrero left the region, returning to Guatemala, and Mazariegos began to encourage local Spaniards to venture into untouched Maya territory. The expansion into these territories was made easier because a large percentage of the local Maya population had been killed.

<u>Rebellion</u>

The main Spanish settlement of Villa Real in the Jovel valley found itself surrounded by an increasingly hostile local Maya population that was constantly fighting for survival. The Spanish forces brought disease to the local Maya and forced them to regularly give up their resources, such as food and water. As famine began to devastate already deteriorating Maya populations, they began to plan a rebellion against the Spaniards. Seeing that Villa Real was now isolated from Spanish reinforcements and supplies, the Maya rose up against their new masters. The only local Maya population that didn't rebel was the city of Zinacantan.

When the local Maya refused to hand over supplies to the colonists of Villa Real, the Spanish led a series of cavalry assaults on the local villages. The Maya withdrew with their families into the remote mountains and caves of the region that served as defensive strongholds. The Spanish and Central Mexican indigenous troops engaged in a head-on battle with the local Maya at Quetzatlepeque, resulting in a Spanish victory despite several casualties. Despite the victory, the rest of the Chiapas population remained hostile to the Spanish.

Mazariegos was soon forced to leave the region due to falling severely ill and was replaced by Juan Enriquez de Guzman as the leader of Villa Real. Guzman attempted to spread Spanish influence throughout the region, but the local population remained noncompliant with the colonial authority.

Ciudad Real

Pedro de Alvarado took over as governor of the Chiapas province in 1531 and immediately renamed Villa Real as San Cristóbal de Los Llanos. A Spanish force attacked the local Maya city of Puyumatlan, and while they were not able to fully take the city, they took many Maya slaves that could be sold in New Spain's growing slave market.

The taking of local slaves became one of the essential parts of the Spanish conquests, as the raiding of small villages usually resulted in few casualties, and slaves could be sold for high prices in the slave market. The capturing of slaves by the conquistadors aided them greatly in their aspirations of conquest, as it created a continuous cycle that made the conquests largely self-funding. Slaves were captured and sold for high prices on the market, and then that money would then be used to buy more horses and weapons, which would be used to capture more slaves and territory. In fact, throughout some periods of the conquest, many conquistadors focused more on conducting small slave-capturing raids on local populations than expanding their territory. However, this obviously contributed to the growing hostility of the local populations.

In 1535, the San Cristóbal de Los Llanos was renamed Ciudad Real, and the colony began to grow into the 1540s as new colonists arrived from throughout New Spain.

Bartolome de Las Casas and the Evangelization of the Chiapas

As the conquests lingered on, many Catholics throughout the Caribbean colonies and Spain began to voice humanitarian concerns about the treatment of the indigenous people of the

Americas. Bartolome de Las Casas became the most prominent critic of the humanitarian disaster unfolding throughout the New World.

Las Casas included this image of the Spanish committing atrocities during the conquest of Cuba in his book. (Credit: Joos van Winghe)

Las Casas was a Spanish priest that helped evangelize indigenous populations during the conquest of the Caribbean. After seeing the horrors of the conquests firsthand, he returned to Europe in 1515 and began campaigning for an investigation that would bring to light the atrocities of the conquistadors. While Las Casas was in favor of colonization and the assimilation of the indigenous people into Spanish Catholic culture, he hoped that he could transform the unchecked genocidal expansion of the Americas into peaceful colonization. One strategy was to send Catholic farmers to the Americas, as they were much more prone to be peaceful colonists than the violent, militant conquistadors.

Las Casas put this strategy to practice in modern-day Venezuela in 1520. He departed Spain with a group of farmers, proclaiming that he would set up a city where the natives and farmers would live peacefully together in an equal, free society. Les Casas hoped to create an alternative to the genocide and exploitation of the conquerors. He hoped to convert the indigenous peoples to Catholicism and at least partially assimilate them into European culture while also giving them the same status as the Spaniards.

However, the plan was doomed from the start. Not only was he only able to recruit a very small number of farmers and laborers to travel to the Americas, but he also met great opposition from local Spanish landlords once they arrived. The town was abandoned in 1522 when it was attacked by nearby indigenous peoples.

After his disastrous experiment in the Americas, Las Casas began writing the Historia de las Indias, which chronicled his experiences during the conquests. The book gave a grim chronicle of the events of the conquests but with a prophetic, religious flavor. The book's main theme prophesized that – one day – Spain would be divinely punished for the horror it brought to the people of the Americas. La Casas made arrangements to make sure that the book would not be published until after his death. Subsequent writings would increasingly have a more secular tone, as he accused the Spaniards of decimating the native population because of their greed for gold and riches.

The Spanish monarchy passed the "New Laws" in 1542, which focused on setting up more officiated administrative systems throughout the conquered regions that would help diminish violence, raiding, and looting against the local populations. This was an immense victory for Las Casas, who King Charles chose to act as the colonial bishop for the Chiapas region.

Las Casas sailed to the Americas in 1544 with a group of followers, arriving in Ciudad Real in March 1545. The arrival of Las Casas and the Dominicans brought sweeping changes to the region's administration, and many local colonists voiced opposition to the new religious interference. The colonists eventually drove the clergy out of Ciudad Real with threats of violence, and they were forced to operate out of nearby rural villages. As the group began evangelizing the region, they eventually moved back into Ciudad Real after tensions with the colonists cooled. However, Las Casas' power as bishop would soon be dismantled by influential colonists who used their power to lobby the Spanish crown.

The New Laws did not succeed in their mission, and King Charles was forced to throw out many of the laws' central provisions. Powerful colonists throughout New Spain threatened rebellion if the laws were enforced, and Charles grew afraid of losing the new American territories he had invested so much in. Despite this, the New Laws served as a monumental moment in the Spanish conquest, as the Spanish Catholic Church, one of the most powerful institutions in the country, began to condemn the brutality of the conquistadors.

After the dissolution of the New Laws, the local colonists increasingly grew hostile to Las Casas, and he was eventually forced to flee the region entirely. After returning to Spain in 1547, he spent the rest of his life writing and preaching about the plight of the indigenous people of the Americas and the devastation caused by the conquests. In the eyes of many indigenous groups, Las Casas would certainly not be a perfect historical figure, as he did advocate for colonization and the conversion of indigenous peoples to Catholicism. However, Las Casas has been celebrated by many Latin American leaders who acknowledge the extraordinary risks he took by speaking out against the powerful conquistadors and the colonial aspirations of the Spanish crown.

Las Casas saw firsthand the moral degradation of the conquests from within and used his power in the Catholic Church to educate the European governments and their populations about the brutal realities of exploration in the New World. Las Casas was one of the first figures to advocate for the native people of the Americas, who were increasingly losing their land, population, and culture to the ever-tightening grip of Spanish colonialism.

Despite the great humanitarian efforts of Las Casas and his fellow Dominican evangelists, these missionaries also went to great lengths to destroy the sacred religious beliefs of the Chiapas Maya. The Dominicans destroyed many sacred Maya temples and monuments throughout the Chiapas region, replacing them with Christian churches.

The missionaries used manipulative tactics to persuade the native population to convert, such as using the biblical book of revelations to convince them that they would be divinely punished if they didn't abandon their own religious beliefs. With the rapid, complete destruction of their lives and livelihoods occurring all around them, it's not hard to understand why so much of the native Maya population began to believe the apocalyptic warnings of the missionaries and convert to Christianity.

Chapter 16: Conquest of the Yucatan Peninsula

As the conquests of the Aztec Empire in Central Mexico were bringing the conquistadors and Spanish crown a massive amount of wealth, the northern Yucatan Peninsula largely stayed on the periphery of colonial ambitions. The fragmented state of the cities and the seemingly impenetrable dense rainforest made the Maya heartland a far less desirable territory to plunder.

Francisco de Montejo

However, in 1526 Francisco de Montejo, a veteran conquistador who helped Cortes conquer the Aztecs, officially received permission from the Spanish crown to conquer the Yucatan. He landed near the village of Xelha in the northeast of the peninsula with 400 men and immediately renamed it "Salamanca de Xelha." The men soon began to run out of food and provisions and increasingly began making raids on local Maya villagers. After the Mayas fled with their food supplies into the rainforest, the men showed signs of declining morale, and Montejo grew concerned that they may hijack a ship and desert. To curb this threat, he burned down all four ships that were docked near the settlement.

The force gradually became accustomed to the harsh conditions of the peninsula and began to spread Spanish influence throughout the northeast Yucatan. In 1528, Montejo and his men arrived in the Maya city of Chaucaca, only to find it completely empty. In the early hours of the morning the following day, the men were ambushed by a force of the city's Maya warriors who had fled to the forest before Montejo's arrival. The Spaniards were able to successfully repulse the attack and immediately departed for the city of Ake. Upon their arrival, a large battle ensued that led to a decisive Spanish victory that left over a thousand Maya warriors dead. After this massive Maya defeat, the local rulers surrendered to Montejo.

After visiting a few other Maya settlements Montejo and his men returned to their base of operations in Xelha, only to find that local Maya killed more than half of the men stationed there. An entire force of Spaniards that were stationed near the village of Pole was also found dead.

After escaping to the Caribbean with his men, in 1529, Montejo became mayor of Tabasco on the Gulf Coast. However, he was not yet finished with his ultimate goal of taking the Yucatan. After several failed attempts to create settlements that would serve as launching points for the conquest of the peninsula, Montejo established a garrison at the city of Campeche. Alonso d' Avila traveled overland throughout the east of the peninsula to form a settlement but was forced to eventually flee to modern-day Honduras due to hostile locals.

A large local Maya military force led an assault on the Spanish troops in Campeche, but Montejo was able to repulse the attack. The local Maya lord, Aj Canul, immediately met with Montejo after the defeat and surrendered. Montejo's son, a high-ranking conquistador by this point, was able to establish the new Spanish colony at the city of Chichen Itza, called Ciudad Real. Some months later, the local Maya ruler was killed during an alleged attempt to assassinate Montejo's son. The death of the Maya ruler further heightened the hostilities between the locals and the Spaniards, and the garrison at Chichen Itza was attacked in the summer of 1533. The Spanish forces were forced to abandon Ciudad Real and flee west to friendlier Maya territories.

The Xiu Maya population in the northwest of the peninsula became the greatest ally of the Spanish during their conquests. Their territory became a safe haven for the conquistadors as they continued attempts to conquer hostile regions. Montejo made a return to Campeche to establish friendlier relations with the Maya there, but rumors of conquistador Francisco Pizarro's expeditions in the Inca heartland in South America began breaking the morale of Montejo's men. While both the conquests of the Aztecs in Central Mexico and the Incas in Peru found enormous wealth, the only thing the Yucatan had brought to the conquistadors were hostile local Maya populations. While the gold uncovered by the initial expeditions was promising, it seemed to many of the Spaniards that they were trying to conquer a civilization that had no wealth or riches worth conquering.

Montejo's men began to desert him for other opportunities in the Americas, and Montejo and his son returned to the Gulf Veracruz region. Montejo and Alvarado engaged in a bitter rivalry over the governorship of Honduras, with Alvarado eventually emerging as the victor.

A Franciscan friar named Jacobo de Testera sailed to the western Yucatan to attempt evangelization and bring the locals into the Spanish Empire peacefully. A loyal friend of fellow evangelist Bartolome de las Casas, Testera had also witnessed firsthand the cruelty of the conquistadors and hoped to bring peaceful colonization to the Yucatan. However, this mission soon fell apart. After arriving in Champoton in 1535, the friar and the conquistadors stationed there became increasingly hostile towards each other, and Testera was forced to abandon his efforts to evangelize the western Yucatan.

After the friar's departure, the Spanish military force in Champoton persuaded the local Maya lords to submit. However, this proved to be a very small victory, as the Spanish garrison was left isolated, surrounded by local populations that had only grown more hostile since their arrival. The bitter reality of the Yucatan conquest disheartened many conquistadors, who increasingly abandoned the prospects of capturing the Maya heartland.

The ruins of a church that had been built with stones from Mayan temples. (Credit: Vmenkov)

The Effects of Conquest on the Maya

After almost twenty years of conquest in the peninsula, the Spaniards now only occupied one isolated outpost on the western coast. While unfathomable amounts of gold and riches were being uncovered throughout the Americas, the Yucatan seemed to be not only one of the most unconquerable regions but also did not have enough wealth to make the conquests worthwhile in the first place.

The Maya heartland, which only a few centuries before had been home to the greatest civilization of the Americas, was increasingly seen as a waste of Spanish resources, lives, and time.

While the Spanish strategized on what to do with the Yucatan, the Maya civilization struggled to survive. Since the Spanish arrived, disease from the Old Word had ravaged their populations. The Spanish's attempts to pit Maya populations against each other worked, and now Maya cities and villages that for centuries considered each other friends, allies, neighbors, and kin increasingly saw each other as potential enemies. While the Maya heartland was never a fully peaceful one, the entrance of the Spanish conquistadors into the fragile, fragmented political ecosystem of the Yucatan created a paranoid environment that inhibited any attempts of unification among the Maya to defend their homeland.

Disease, famine, and political manipulation had permanently ruptured any semblance of Maya unification, as each city and village began fighting for its survival in the new destructive landscape created by the Spanish conquests. All the Maya could do now was hold on to their cultural systems that were still firmly in place and anticipate the next arrival of the conquistadors in the northern Yucatan.

The Colonization of the Northern Yucatan

Montejo's son, Montejo the Younger, took over the colonization of the northern Yucatan from his father in 1540. The next year, he brought his troops first to Champoton and then to Campeche, where he created the Yucatan's first local colonial town council. Montejo the Younger knew that to avoid the mistakes of the earlier conquests of the peninsula, he had to create stable local administrative power structures that would attract colonists and create a permanent Spanish colonial presence in the region. After creating the council, he approached the local Maya settlements and ordered them to surrender, which many local lords agreed to.

However, the local Canul Maya ruler remained hostile, and Montejo the Younger sent his cousin to their city. The second colonial town council, Merida, was created near the Canul city, and the Spanish troops garrisoned there were approached by the Canul lord. He hoped to establish peace with the Spaniards. The ruler, Tutul Xiu, was awestruck by the priests when they Catholic mass and immediately converted to Christianity.

The submission of Tutul Xiu to the Spanish at Merida was one of the most important moments of the Yucatan conquest. Tutul Xiu was one of the most influential rulers of the Maya world, and his surrender created a domino effect, as Maya rulers throughout the west Yucatan began to submit to Spanish colonial authority. While the rulers of the eastern Yucatan remained hostile to the Spanish, the increasing influence in the west gave the Spaniards the breathing-room and native allies they needed to fully conquer the entirety of the Maya heartland.

Spanish forces were sent eastward, where many rulers accepted the Spaniards peacefully, and those that didn't were swiftly defeated. As these forces reached the far-east Yucatan Maya, many remained hostile and were able to stay independent from Spanish authority. However, by 1546 the Spanish had much of the western and central parts of the northern Yucatan firmly under their control.

In November 1546, the most powerful Maya lords of the independent eastern regions conducted a massive, well-organized rebellion against the Spanish colonial authorities. Garrisons and colonial settlements throughout the west were attacked by Maya warriors, leading to heavy casualties on both sides. The Maya were eventually defeated in a final climactic battle, and much of the population of the western provinces fled southwards to the central and southern lowlands. After 30 years of conquest, the Spanish had finally captured the northern Yucatan.

Chapter 17: The Final Conquests

With the northern Yucatan and most of the highlands now firmly under Spanish control, the central and southern lowlands, namely the Peten Basin, became the last surviving independent Maya region. Thousands of Maya from throughout the region continually poured into the region to escape famine, disease, slavery, and the colonial system. The Spanish saw this as a massive threat, as their encomienda system was heavily reliant on the labor of indigenous locals.

This region would be – by far – the most unconquerable territory of all of Central America. Aside from the dense rainforests, there were very freshwater sources to sustain a military force during campaigns, and settlements tended to be somewhat isolated. The people of the region, especially the Itza Maya, were the fiercest warriors the Spanish had yet encountered in the Americas.

By the mid-16th century, the Itza had learned many of the tactics of the Spanish from the migrants who fled the northern Yucatan and the highlands and began to use their terrain to their advantage by using hit-and-run tactics on the conquistadors. Due to the region's dense forest, the Spanish were robbed of their greatest military advantage: the use of cavalry. However, the decline of trade in the region and the increased isolation of Itza communities meant that it was only a matter of time before they too fell to the Spanish.

As covered in Chapter 12, the conquest of the Peten Basin began with the arrival of the missionaries during the mid-16th century. The city of Nojpeten was the final major Maya city to fall to the Spanish, finally being conquered in March 1697. The region held out for over 150 years after the initial Yucatan conquests.

After centuries of progression from the Olmec cities on the Gulf Coast to the city centers of the lowlands, the great Maya civilization now found itself fully at the mercy of the Spanish colonial government.

Conclusion

The complete conquest of the Maya heartland would not be the end of the hardship for the Maya people. In fact, it was only the beginning. From the Spanish crown to the modern Guatemalan government, the Maya people would experience many years of exploitation and oppression.

So, what can be learned about the Maya civilization, and how can those lessons be used in a modern context? How do the stone step pyramids have anything to do with the modern skyscrapers of our great cities like New York City or Dubai? How could an ancient belief system comprised of mythical gods have anything to do with 21st-century life? While the Maya civilization of the Yucatan Peninsula may seem too distant in the past to draw modern lessons from, the 21st-century international landscape serves as a direct reflection of the ancient Maya political system.

The Maya had long-distance trade routes throughout the Yucatan that created a complex economy within Central America, greatly mirroring the international trade systems of today. How could one study the conflict between Tikal and Calakmul and not think about the U.S.-Soviet Cold War, where each side fought proxy wars and created alliance systems to gain political dominance? While modern international studies dwarf that of the

Maya, nearly every theme of the 21ˢᵗ-century international order can be seen within the Maya civilization within a relatively small area on the Yucatan Peninsula.

Many of the international problems society faces today, from war to income inequality, to environmental degradation, are often looked at as modern problems. The threats that the Maya civilization faced show that many of these problems are not solely born out of the 21ˢᵗ century. Instead, they are human problems that have been a part of our history since the beginning of time. Thus, instead of condemning the lessons of ancient civilizations of the past as "too old to be relevant," we should study the problems they faced and how they combatted them.

Inherent in the Maya belief system was time. The Maya were not only fascinated with it; they were obsessed with it. Time was studied largely through astronomical observation and record-keeping to keep track of agricultural seasons, conduct religious ceremonies, and many other time-reliant necessities.

The central idea revolving around time for the Maya was their belief that their universe would eventually be destroyed by the gods and replaced anew by another. Out of all their astoundingly astronomical and mathematical theories, their breathtaking architecture that is still marveled at today, their lively cultural practices and art that could compete with anything that was being produced in contemporary Europe, perhaps their concept of the "destruction of the universe" was the one thing that the Maya got wrong.

The survival and thriving of the Maya people of today show that universes, worlds, and civilizations are never truly destroyed. Instead, history goes through a cyclical pattern of destruction, dispersal, and creation that combines the remnants of the old with the inventions of the new.

Though the decline of Tikal and Calakmul meant the destruction of a peninsula-wide political system and the great urban centers of the era, their populations brought the remnants of what made these cities great to other regions. There, the Maya populations learned from the errors of the great lowland urban centers and expanded upon them. Though the Spanish conquistadors ravaged the Yucatan with their aspirations of conquest and evangelization, the Maya people firmly held on to their culture and history. Though the nearby cities and towns may have Spanish names and spoken language, the Maya have found their place in modern Central American life while also keeping a firm hold on to their cultural heritage.

The Maya civilization never collapsed, nor did it die out due to the brutal conquests of the conquistadors; the Maya civilization has survived to the present day despite the apocalyptic collapse of the Terminal Classic and the conquests of the 16th century. The survival of the Maya has shown that no matter how apocalyptic a threat may be, a strong, resilient cultural foundation will stay strong in its people.

It is hard not to point out the bitter irony that as Catholicism is declining amongst the population of Spain today, the traditional culture of the rural Maya peoples has remained an inherent, inexorable part of their lives. Though the immense brutality of the Spanish conquests and collapse of the Maya city-states may not show it, it is clear that the gods of the Maya are still watching over their people of the Yucatan today.

Here's another book by Enthralling History that you might be interested in

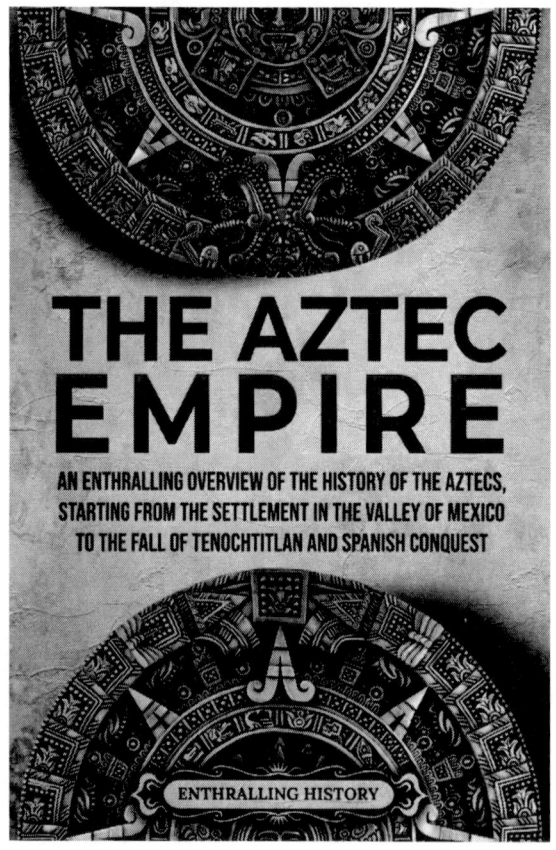

Free limited time bonus

Stop for a moment. We have a free bonus set up for you. The problem is this: we forget 90% of everything that we read after 7 days. Crazy fact, right? Here's the solution: we've created a printable, 1-page pdf summary for this book that you're reading now. All you have to do to get your free pdf summary is to go to the following website: **https://livetolearn.lpages.co/enthrallinghistory/**

Once you do, it will be intuitive. Enjoy, and thank you!

Bibliography:

David Freidel. A Forest of Kings: The Untold Story of the Ancient Maya. William Morrow Paperbacks; January 24, 1992.

Matthew Restall. Invading Guatemala: Spanish, Nahua, and Maya Accounts of the Conquest Wars. Penn State University Press; January 15, 2008.

Lawrence H. Feldman. Lost Shores, Forgotten Peoples: Spanish Explorations of the South East Maya Lowlands. Duke University Press Books; February 5, 2001.

David Drew. The Lost Chronicles of the Maya Kings. University of California Press; March 20, 2000.

Elliot M. Abrams. How the Maya Built Their World: Energetics and Ancient Architecture. University of Texas Press; June 4, 2010.

Simon Martin, Nikolai Grube. Chronicle of the Maya Kings and Queens: Deciphering The Dynasties of the Ancient Maya. Thames & Hudson; April 28, 2008.

Michael D. Coe, Stephen D. Houston. The Maya (Ancient Peoples and Places). Thames & Hudson; June 16, 2015.

Richard Diehl. Olmecs: America's First Civilization (Ancient Peoples & Places). Thames and Hudson; December 31, 2004.

Michael D. Coe. America's First Civilization. Discovering the Olmec. American Heritage Association / Smithsonian; January 1, 1968.

Robert M. Rosenswig. The Beginnings of Mesoamerican Civilization: Inter-Regional Interaction and the Olmec. Cambridge University Press; December 28, 2009.

Francisco Estrada-Belli. The First Maya Civilization: Ritual and Power Before the Classic Period. Routledge; December 20, 2010.

Sarah E. Jackson. Politics of the Maya Court: Hierarchy and Change in the Late Classic Period. University of Oklahoma Press. May 24, 2013.

Made in United States
North Haven, CT
11 December 2023

45544573R00096